Waiting on God and Absolute Surrender

Waiting on God

and

Absolute Surrender

Andrew Murray

SURREY, BRITISH COLUMBIA
EREMITICAL PRESS

Contents

ABSOLUTE SURRENDER

Waiting on God

Preface

Previous to my leaving home for England last year, I had been much impressed by the thought of how, in all our religion, personal and public, we need more of God. I had felt that we needed to train our people in their worship more to wait on God, and to make the cultivation of a deeper sense of his presence—of more direct contact with him, of entire dependence on him—a definite aim of our ministry. At a "welcome" breakfast in Exeter Hall, I gave very simple expression to this thought in connection with all our religious work. I have already said elsewhere that I was surprised at the response, the sentiment met with. I saw that God's Spirit had been working the same desire in many hearts.

The experiences of the past year, both personal and public, have greatly deepened the conviction. It is as if I myself am only beginning to see the deepest truth concerning God and our relation to him center in this waiting on God, and how very little, in our life and work, we have been surrounded by its spirit. The following pages are the outcome of my conviction, and of the desire to direct the attention of all God's people to the one great remedy for all our needs. More than half the pieces were written on board ship; I fear they bear the marks of being somewhat crude and hasty. I have felt, in looking them over, as if I could wish to write them over again. But this I cannot now do. And so I send them out with the prayer that he who loves to use the feeble may give his blessing with them.

I do not know if it will be possible for me to put into a few words what are the chief things we need to learn. In a note at the close of the book on William Law, I have mentioned some. But what I want to say here is this: The great lack of our religion is, we do not know God. The answer to every complaint of feebleness and failure, the message to every congregation or convention seeking instruction on holiness, ought to be simply: "What is the matter? Have you not God? If you really believe in God, he will put all right. God is willing and able by his Holy Spirit. Cease from expecting the least good from yourself, or the least help from anything there is in man, and just yield yourself unreservedly to God to work in you. He will do all for you."

How simple this looks! And yet this is the gospel we so little know. I feel ashamed as I send forth these very defective meditations; I can only cast them on the love of my brethren and of our God. May he use them to draw us all to himself, to learn in practice and experience the blessed art of waiting only upon God. Would God that we might get some right conception of what the influence would be of a life given, not in thought or imagination or effort, but in the power of the Holy Spirit, wholly to waiting upon God.

With my greeting in Christ to all God's saints it has been my privilege to meet, and no less to those I have not met, I subscribe myself, your brother and servant,

ANDREW MURRAY
WELLINGTON
MARCH 3, 1896

P. S.   In this little book I have more than once spoken of our waiting on God in our Conventions. I have been much interested in noticing in the life of Canon Battersly how prominent the thought was in his mind. In a paper preparing the way for Keswick, he speaks of three steps needful to the attainment of true holiness. The two first are a clear view of the possibilities of Christian attainment, and a deliberate purpose to live the life. And then the third: "We must look up to, and wait upon our ascended Lord for all that we need to enable us to do this." In a letter written a few days after the first Keswick Convention in 1875, he writes again: "At the first meeting the keynote was struck which vibrated through all our meetings: 'My soul! Wait only upon God, for my expectation is from him.'" And farther, "There is a very remarkable resemblance in all the testimonies which I have since received, viz., the ability given to make a full surrender to the Lord, and the consequent experience of an abiding peace."

The God of Our Salvation

My soul waits only upon God; from him comes my salvation.
—*Psalm 62:1*

If salvation indeed comes from God, and is entirely his work, just as our creation was, it follows as a matter of course that our first and highest duty is to wait on him to do that work as it pleases him. Waiting becomes, then, the only way to the experience of a full salvation—the only way truly to know God as the God of our salvation. All the difficulties that are brought forward as keeping us back from full salvation have their cause in this one thing: the defective knowledge and practice of waiting upon God. All that the Church and its members need for the manifestation of the mighty power of God in the world is the return to our true place, the place that belongs to us both in creation and redemption, the place of absolute and unceasing dependence upon God. Let us strive to see what the elements are that make up this most blessed and needful waiting upon God: it may help us to discover the reasons why this grace is so little cultivated, and to feel how infinitely desirable it is that the Church, and that we ourselves, should at any price learn its blessed secret.

The deep need for this waiting on God lies equally in the nature of man and the nature of God. God, as Creator, formed man, to be a vessel in which he could show forth his power and goodness. Man was not to have in himself a fountain of life or strength or happiness: the ever living and only living One was, each moment, to be the Communicator to him of all that he needed. Man's glory and blessedness was not to be independent, or dependent upon himself, but dependent on a God of such infinite riches and love. Man was to have the joy of receiving every moment out of the fullness of God. This was his blessedness as an unfallen creature.

When he fell from God, he was still more absolutely dependent on him. There was not the slightest hope of his recovery out of his state of death, but in God, his power and mercy. It is God alone who began the work of redemption; it is God alone who continues and carries it on, each moment, in each individual believer. Even in the regenerate man, there is no power of goodness in himself: he has and can have nothing that he does not each moment receive; and waiting on God is just as indispensable, and must be just as continuous and unbroken, as the breathing that maintains his natural life.

It is only because Christians do not know in their relation to God of their own absolute poverty and helplessness that they have no sense of the need of absolute and unceasing dependence, or of the unspeakable blessedness of continual waiting on God. But when once a believer begins to see it and consent to it—that he by the Holy Spirit must each moment receive what God each moment works—waiting on God becomes his brightest hope and joy. As he appreciates how God, as God, as Infinite Love, delights to impart his own nature to his child as fully as he can, how God is not weary of each moment keeping charge of his life and strength, he wonders that he ever thought otherwise of God than as a God to be waited on all the day. God unceasingly giving and working; his child unceasingly waiting and receiving: this is the blessed life.

"Truly my soul waits upon God; from him comes my salvation." First we wait on God for salvation. Then we learn that salvation is only to bring us to God, and teach us to wait on him. Then we find what is better still: that waiting on God is itself the highest salvation. It is the ascribing to him the glory of being All; it is the experiencing that he is All to us. May God teach us the blessedness of waiting on him.

My soul, wait only upon God!

The Keynote of Life

I have waited for your salvation, O Lord!
—*Genesis 49:18*

It is not easy to say exactly in what sense Jacob used these words in the midst of his prophecies in regard to the future of his sons. But they do certainly indicate that both for himself and for them, his expectation was from God alone. It was God's salvation he waited for; a salvation which God had promised and which God himself alone could work out. He knew himself and his sons to be under God's charge. Jehovah the Everlasting God would show in them what his saving power is and does. The words point forward to that wonderful history of redemption which is not yet finished, and to the glorious future in eternity where it is leading. They suggest to us how there is no salvation but God's salvation, and how waiting on God for that, whether for our personal experience or in wider circles, is our first duty, our true blessedness.

Let us think of ourselves, and the inconceivably glorious salvation God has wrought for us in Christ, and is now purposing to work out and to perfect in us by his Spirit. Let us meditate until we somewhat realize that every participation of this great salvation, from moment to moment, must be the work of God himself. God cannot part with his grace, or goodness, or strength, as an external thing that he gives us, as he gives the raindrops from heaven. No; he can only give it, and we can only enjoy it, as he works it himself directly and unceasingly. And the only reason that he does not work it more effectively and continuously is that we do not let him. We hinder him either by our indifference or by our self-effort, so that he cannot do what he would. What he asks of us, in the way of surrender and obedience and desire and trust, is all comprised in this one word: waiting on him; waiting for his salvation. It combines the deep sense of our entire helplessness of ourselves to work what is divinely good, and the perfect assurance that our God will work it all in his divine power.

Again, I say, let us meditate on the divine glory of the salvation God purposes working out in us, until we know the truth it implies. Our heart is the scene of a divine operation more wonderful than Creation. We can do as little towards the work as towards creating the world, except as God works in us to will and to do. God only asks of us to yield, to consent, to wait upon him, and he will do it all. Let us meditate and be still, until we see how appropriate and right and blessed it is that God alone do all, and our soul will of itself sink down in deep humility to say: "I have waited for your salvation, O Lord." And the deep, blessed background of all our praying and working will be, "Truly my soul waits upon God."

The application of the truth to wider circles, to those we labor among or intercede for, to the Church of Christ around us, or throughout the world, is not difficult. There can be no good but what God works; to wait upon God, and have the heart filled with faith in his working, and in that faith to pray for his mighty power to come down, is our only wisdom. Oh, for the eyes of our heart to be opened to see God working in ourselves and in others, and to see how blessed it is to worship and just to wait for his salvation!

Our private and public prayer are our chief expression of our relation to God: it is in them chiefly that our waiting upon God must be exercised. If our waiting begins by quieting the activities of nature and being still before God; if it bows and seeks to see God in his universal and almighty operation, alone able and always ready to work all good; if it yields itself to him in the assurance that he is working and will work in us; if it maintains the place of humility and stillness and surrender, until God's Spirit has quickened the faith that he will perfect his work: it will indeed become the strength and the joy of the soul. Life will become one deep, blessed cry: "I have waited for your salvation, O Lord."

My soul, wait only upon God!

DAY 3

The True Place of the Creature

These all wait all upon you; that you may give them their
meat in due season. That you give them, they gather;
you open your hand, they are filled with good.
—*Psalm 104:27-28*

This Psalm, in praise of the Creator, has been speaking of the birds and
the beasts of the forest; of the young lions, and man going forth to his
work; of the great sea, wherein are things creeping innumerable, both
small and great beasts. And it sums up the whole relation of all creation
to its Creator, and its continuous and universal dependence upon him
in the one word: "These all wait upon you!" Just as much as it was God's
work to create, it is his work to maintain. As little as the creature could
create itself, is it left to provide for itself. The whole creation is ruled by
the one unalterable law of waiting upon God!

The word is the simple expression of that for the sake of which alone
the creature was brought into existence, the very groundwork of its constitution. The one object for which God gave life to creatures was that in
them he might prove and show forth his wisdom, power, and goodness,
in his being each moment their life and happiness, and pouring forth unto
them, according to their capacity, the riches of his goodness and power.
And just as this is the very place and nature of God—to be unceasingly
the supplier of every want in the creature—so the very place and nature
of the creature is nothing but this: to wait upon God and receive from
him what he alone can give, what he delights to give.

If we are in this little book at all to appreciate what waiting on God is to be to the believer, to practice it and to experience its blessedness, it is of consequence that we begin at the very beginning, and see the deep reasonableness of the call that comes to us. We shall understand how the duty is no arbitrary command. We shall see how it is not only rendered necessary by our sin and helplessness; it is simply and truly our restoration to our original destiny and our highest nobility, to our true place and glory as creatures blessedly dependent on the All-Glorious God.

If once our eyes are opened to this precious truth, all Nature will become a preacher, reminding us of the relationship which, founded in creation, is now taken up in grace. As we read this Psalm, and learn to look upon all life in Nature as continually maintained by God himself, waiting on God will be seen to be the very necessity of our being. As we think of the young lions and the ravens crying to him, of the birds and the fish and every insect waiting on him, until he give them their meat in due season, we shall see that it is the very nature and glory of God that he is a God who is to be waited on. Every thought of what Nature is, and what God is, will give new force to the call, "Wait only upon God."

"These all wait upon you, that you may give." It is God who gives all: let this faith enter deeply into our hearts. Before we fully understand all that is implied in our waiting upon God, and before we ever have been able to cultivate the habit, let the truth enter our souls: waiting on God, unceasing and entire dependence upon him, is, in heaven and earth, the one and only true religion, the one unalterable and all-comprehensive expression for the true relationship to the ever-blessed One in whom we live.

Let us resolve at once that it shall be the one characteristic of our life and worship, a continual, humble, trustful waiting upon God. We may rest assured that he who made us for himself, that he might give himself to us and in us, that he will never disappoint us. In waiting on him we shall find rest and joy and strength, and the supply of every need.

My soul, wait only upon God!

DAY 4

For Supplies

*The Lord upholds all that fall, and raises up all those that
are bowed down. The eyes of all wait upon you;
and you give them their meat in due season.*
—*Psalm 145:14–15*

Psalm 104 is a Psalm of Creation, and the words, "These all wait upon you," were used with reference to the animal creation. Here we have a Psalm of the Kingdom, and "The eyes of all wait upon you" appears especially to point to the needs of God's saints, of all that fall, and them that be bowed down. What the universe and the animal creation does unconsciously, God's people are to do intelligently and voluntarily. Man is to be the interpreter of Nature. He is to prove that there is nothing more noble or more blessed in the exercise of our free will than to use it in waiting upon God.

If an army has been sent out to march into an enemy's country, and tidings are received that it is not advancing, the question is at once asked, "What may be the cause of delay?" The answer will very often be, "Waiting for supplies." All the stores of provisions or clothing or ammunition have not arrived; without these it dare not proceed. It is not otherwise in the Christian life: day by day, at every step, we need our supplies from above. And there is nothing so needful as to cultivate that spirit of dependence on God and of confidence in him, which refuses to go on without the needed supply of grace and strength.

If the question be asked, whether this be anything different from what we do when we pray, the answer is that there may be much praying with but very little waiting on God. In praying we are often occupied with ourselves, with our own needs, and our own efforts in the presentation of them. In waiting upon God, the first thought is of the God upon whom we wait. We enter his presence, and feel we need just to be quiet, so that he, as God, can overshadow us with himself. God longs to reveal himself, to fill us with himself. Waiting on God gives him time in his own way, and divine power to come to us.

It is especially at the time of prayer that we ought to set ourselves to cultivate this spirit. Before you pray, bow quietly before God, and seek to remember and realize who he is, how near he is, how certainly he can and will help. Just be still before him, and allow his Holy Spirit to awaken and stir up in your soul the childlike disposition of absolute dependence and confident expectation. Wait upon God as a Living Being, as the Living God, who notices you, and is just longing to fill you with his salvation. Wait on God until you know you have met him; prayer will then become so different.

And when you are praying, let there be intervals of silence, reverent stillness of soul, in which you yield yourself to God, in case he may have aught he wishes to teach you or to work in you. Waiting on him will become the most blessed part of prayer, and the blessing thus obtained will be doubly precious as the fruit of such fellowship with the Holy One. God has so ordained it, in harmony with his holy nature, and with ours, that waiting on him should be the honor we give him. Let us bring him the service gladly and truthfully; he will reward it abundantly.

"The eyes of all wait upon you, and you give them their meat in due season." Dear soul, God provides in Nature for the creatures he has made; how much more will he provide in Grace for those he has redeemed? Learn to say of every want, and every failure, and every lack of needful grace: I have waited too little upon God, or he would have given me in due season all I needed. And say then, too:

My soul, wait only upon God!

DAY 5

For Instruction

Show me your ways, O Lord; Teach me your paths.
Lead me in your truth, and teach me: for you are the God
of my salvation; on you do I wait all the day.
—*Psalm 25:4–5*

I spoke of an army, on the point of entering an enemy's territories, answering the question as to the cause of delay: "Waiting for supplies." The answer might also have been, "Waiting for instructions," or, "Waiting for orders." If the last despatch had not been received, with the final orders of the commander-in-chief, the army dared not move. Even so in the Christian life: as deep as the need of waiting for supplies is that of waiting for instructions.

See how beautifully this comes out in Psalm 25. The writer knew and loved God's law exceedingly, and meditated on that law day and night. But he knew that this was not enough. He knew that for the right spiritual understanding of the truth, and for the right personal application of it to his own peculiar circumstances, he needed a direct, divine teaching.

The psalm has at all times been a very favorite one because of its reiterated expression of the felt need of the Divine teaching, and of the childlike confidence that that teaching would be given. Study the psalm until your heart is filled with the two thoughts: the absolute need, and the absolute certainty, of divine guidance. And notice, then, how entirely it is in this connection that he speaks, "On you do I wait all the day." Waiting for guidance, waiting for instruction, all the day, is a very blessed part of waiting upon God.

The Father in heaven is so interested in his child, and so longs to have his life at every step in his will and his love, that he is willing to keep his guidance entirely in his own hand. He knows so well that we are unable to do what is really holy and heavenly, except as he works it in us, that he means his very demands to become promises of what he will do, in watching over and leading us all the day. Not only in special difficulties and times of perplexity, but in the common course of everyday life, we may count upon him to teach us his way, and show us his path.

And what is needed in us to receive this guidance? One thing: waiting for instructions, waiting on God. "On you do I wait all the day." We want, in our times of prayer, to give clear expression to our sense of need, and our faith in his help. We want definitely to become conscious of our ignorance as to what God's way may be, and the need of the Divine light shining within us, if our way is to be as of the sun, shining more and more unto the perfect day. And we want to wait quietly before God in prayer, until the deep, restful assurance fills us: It will be given: "The meek will he guide in the way."

"On you do I wait all the day." The special surrender to the Divine guidance in our seasons of prayer must cultivate, and be followed up by, the habitual looking upwards "all the day." As simple as it is, to one who has eyes, to walk all the day in the light of the sun, so simple and delightful can it become to a soul practiced in waiting on God, to walk all the day in the enjoyment of God's light and leading. What is needed to help us to such a life is just one thing: the real knowledge and faith of God as the one only source of wisdom and goodness, as ever ready, and longing much to be to us all that we can possibly require. Yes! This is the one thing we need. If we but saw our God in his love, if we but believed that he waits to be gracious, that he waits to be our life and to work all in us, how this waiting on God would become our highest joy, the natural and spontaneous response of our hearts to his great love and glory!

O God! Teach us, above everything, the blessed lesson, that all the day, and every moment of it, you are around and within us, working out your work of love. Show us that you only ask of us that we wait on you. And so teach us to say, "on you do I wait all the day."

My soul, wait only upon God!

DAY 6

For All Saints

Let none that wait on you be ashamed.
—*Psalm 25:3*

Let us now, in our meditation of today, each one forget himself, to think of the great company of God's saints throughout the world, who are all with us waiting on him. And let us all join in the fervent prayer for each other, "Let none that wait on you be ashamed."

Just think for a moment of the multitude of waiting ones who need that prayer: how many there are, sick and weary and solitary, to whom it is as if their prayers are not answered, and who sometimes begin to fear that their hope will be put to shame. And then, how many servants of God, ministers or missionaries, teachers or workers, of various names, whose hopes in their work have been disappointed, and whose longing for power and blessing remains unsatisfied. And then, too, how many, who have heard of a life of rest and perfect peace, of abiding light and fellowship, of strength and victory, and who cannot find the path. With all these, it is nothing but that they have not yet learned the secret of full waiting upon God. They just need what we all need: the living assurance that waiting on God can never be in vain. Let us remember all who are in danger of fainting or being weary, and all unite in the cry, "Let none that wait on you be ashamed!"

If this intercession for all who wait on God becomes part of our waiting on him for ourselves, we shall help to bear each other's burdens, and so fulfill the law of Christ. There will be introduced into our waiting on God that element of unselfishness and love, which is the path to the highest blessing, and the fullest communion with God. Love to the brethren and love to God are inseparably linked. In God, the love to his Son and to us are one: "That the love, wherewith you have loved me, may be in them." In Christ, the love of the Father to him, and his love to us, are one: "As the Father loved me, so have I loved you." In us, he asks that his love to us shall be ours to the brethren: "As I have loved you, that you love one another." All the love of God, and of Christ, are inseparably linked with love to the brethren. And how can we, day by day, prove and cultivate this love otherwise than by daily praying for each other? Christ did not seek to enjoy the Father's love for himself: he passed it all on to us. All true seeking of God and his love for ourselves will be inseparably linked with the thought and the love of our brethren in prayer for them.

"Let none that wait on you be ashamed." Twice in the psalm, David speaks of his waiting on God for himself; here he thinks of all who wait on him. Let this page take the message to all God's tried and weary ones, that there are more praying for them than they know. Let it stir them and us in our waiting to make a point of at times forgetting ourselves, and to enlarge our hearts, and say to the Father, "These all wait upon you, and you give them their meat in due season." Let it inspire us all with new courage. For who is there who is not at times ready to faint and be weary? "Let none that wait on you be ashamed" is a promise in a prayer: "They that wait on you shall not be ashamed!" From many and many a witness the cry comes to everyone who needs the help, brother, sister, tried one: "Wait on the Lord; be of good courage, and he shall strengthen your heart; wait, I say, on the Lord. Be of good courage, and he shall strengthen your heart, all you that wait on the Lord."

Blessed Father! We humbly beseech you, let none that wait on you be ashamed; no, not one. Some are weary, and the time of waiting appears long. And some are feeble, and scarcely know how to wait. And some are so entangled in the effort of their prayers and their work, they think that they can find no time to wait continually. Father, teach us all how to wait. Teach us to think of each other, and pray for each other. Teach us to think of you, the God of all waiting ones. Father, let none that wait on you be ashamed. For Jesus' sake. Amen."

My soul, wait only upon God!

DAY 7

A Plea in Prayer

Let integrity and uprightness preserve me; for I wait on you.
—*Psalm 25:21*

For the third time in this psalm, we have the word "wait." As before, in verse 5, "On you do I wait all the day," so here, too, the believing supplicant appeals to God to remember that he is waiting on him, looking for an answer. It is a great thing for a soul not only to wait upon God, but to be filled with such a consciousness that its whole spirit and position is that of a waiting one; that it can, in childlike confidence, say, "Lord, you know I wait on you." It will prove a mighty plea in prayer, giving ever-increasing boldness of expectation to claim the promise, "They that wait on me shall not be ashamed!"

The prayer in connection with which the plea is put forth here is one of great importance in the spiritual life. If we draw near to God, it must be with a true heart. There must be perfect integrity, whole-heartedness, in our dealing with God. As we read in the next psalm, "Judge me, O Lord, for I have walked in my integrity" (Psalm 26:1) and "As for me, I will walk in my integrity" (Psalm 26:11), there must be perfect uprightness or single-heartedness before God. As it is written, "His righteousness is for the upright in heart." The soul must know that it allows nothing sinful, nothing doubtful; if it is indeed to meet the Holy One, and receive his full blessing, it must be with a heart wholly and singly given up to his will. The whole spirit that animates us in the waiting must be, "Let integrity and uprightness." You see that I desire to come so to you; you know I am looking to you to work them perfectly in me—let them "preserve me, for I wait on you."

And if, at our first attempt truly to live the life of fully and always waiting on God, we begin to discover how much that perfect integrity is wanting, this will just be one of the blessings which the waiting was meant to work. A soul cannot seek close fellowship with God, or attain the abiding consciousness of waiting on him all the day, without a very honest and entire surrender to all his will.

"For I wait on you." It is not only in connection with the prayer of our text, but with every prayer that this plea may be used. To use it often will be a great blessing to ourselves. Let us therefore study the words well until we know all their bearings. It must be clear to us what we are waiting for. There may be very different things. It may be waiting for God in our times of prayer to take his place as God, and to work in us the sense of his holy presence and nearness. It may be some special petition, to which we are expecting an answer. It may be our whole inner life, in which we are on the lookout for God's putting forth of his power. It may be the whole state of his Church and saints, or some part of his work, for which our eyes are ever toward him. It is good that we sometimes count up to ourselves exactly what the things are we are waiting for, and as we say definitely of each of them, "On you do I wait," we shall be emboldened to claim the answer, "For on you do I wait."

It must also be clear to us on whom we are waiting. Not an idol, a God of whom we have made an image by our conceptions of what he is. No, but the living God, such as he really is in his great glory, his infinite holiness, his power, wisdom, and goodness, in his love and nearness. It is the presence of a beloved or a dreaded master that wakens up the whole attention of the servant who waits on him. It is the presence of God, as he can in Christ by his Holy Spirit make himself known, and keep the soul under its covering and shadow, that will awaken and strengthen the true waiting spirit. Let us be still and wait and worship until we know how near he is, and then say, "On you do I wait."

And then, let it be very clear, too, that we are waiting. Let that become so much our consciousness that the utterance comes spontaneously, "On you I do wait all the day; I wait on you." This will indeed imply sacrifice and separation, a soul entirely given up to God as its all, its only joy. This waiting on God has hardly yet been acknowledged as the only true Christianity. And yet, if it be true that God alone is goodness and joy and love; if it be true that our highest blessedness is in having as much of God as we can; if it be true that Christ has redeemed us wholly for God, and made a life of continual abiding in his presence possible, nothing less ought to satisfy than to be ever breathing this blessed atmosphere, "I wait on you."

My soul, wait only on God!

Strong and of Good Courage

Wait on the Lord: be strong, and let your heart take courage;
yea, wait on the Lord.
—*Psalm 27:14*

The psalmist had just said, "I had fainted, unless I had believed to see the goodness of the Lord in the land of the living." If it had not been for his faith in God, his heart would have fainted. But in the confident assurance in God which faith gives, he urges himself and us to remember one thing above all, to wait upon God. "Wait on the Lord: be strong, and let your heart take courage: yea, wait on the Lord." One of the chief needs in our waiting upon God, one of the deepest secrets of its blessedness and blessing, is a quiet, confident persuasion that it is not in vain; courage to believe that God will hear and help; that we are waiting on a God who never could disappoint his people.

"Be strong and of good courage." These words are frequently found in connection with some great and difficult enterprise, in prospect of the combat with the power of strong enemies, and the utter insufficiency of all human strength. Is waiting on God a work so difficult, that, for that too, such words are needed, "Be strong, and let your heart take courage"? Yes, indeed. The deliverance, for which we often have to wait, is from enemies, in the presence of whom we are impotent. The blessings for which we plead are spiritual and all unseen; things impossible with men; heavenly, supernatural, divine realities. Our souls are so little accustomed to hold fellowship with God that the God on whom we wait so often appears to hide himself. We who have to wait are often tempted to fear that we do not wait aright, that our faith is too feeble, that our desire is not as upright or as earnest as it should be, and that our surrender is not complete. Our heart may well faint and fail; amid all these causes of fear or doubt, how blessed to hear the voice of God: "Wait on the Lord! Be strong, and let your heart take courage!" Yes, wait on the Lord! Let nothing in heaven or earth or hell—let nothing keep you from waiting on your God in full assurance that it cannot be in vain.

The one lesson our text teaches us is, thus, that when we set ourselves to wait on God, we ought beforehand to resolve that it shall be with the most confident expectation of God's meeting and blessing us. We ought to make up our minds to this, that nothing was ever so sure as that waiting on God will bring us untold and unexpected blessing. We are so accustomed to judge of God and his work in us by what we feel that the great probability is that when we begin more to cultivate the waiting on him, we shall be discouraged, because we do not find any special blessing from it. The message comes to us: "Above everything, when you wait on God, do so in the spirit of abounding hopefulness. It is God in his glory, in his power, in his love longing to bless you that you are waiting on."

If you say that you are afraid of deceiving yourself with vain hope, because you do not see or feel any warrant in your present state for such special expectations, my answer is, it is God who is the warrant for your expecting great things. Oh, do learn the lesson. You are not going to wait on yourself to see what you feel and what changes come to you. You are going to wait on God, to know first, what he is, and then, after that, what he will do. The whole duty and blessedness of waiting on God has its root in this: that he is such a blessed Being, full to overflowing of goodness and power and life and joy, that we, however wretched, cannot for any time come into contact with him, without that life and power secretly, silently beginning to enter into us and blessing us. God is Love! That is the one, only, and all-sufficient warrant of your expectation. Love seeks not its own. God's love is just his delight to impart himself and his blessedness to his children. Come, and however feeble you feel, just wait in his presence. As a feeble, sickly invalid is brought out into the sunshine to let its warmth go through him, come with all that is dark and cold in you into the sunshine of God's holy, omnipotent love, and sit and wait there, with the one thought: Here I am, in the sunshine of his love. As the sun does its work in the weak one who seeks its rays, God will do his work in you. Oh, do trust him fully. "Wait on the Lord! Be strong, and let your heart take courage! Yes, wait on the Lord!"

My soul, wait only upon God!

DAY 9

With the Heart

Be strong, and let your heart take courage,
all you that wait for the Lord.
—*Psalm 31:24*

The words are nearly the same as in our last meditation. But I gladly avail
myself of them again to press home a much-needed lesson for all who
desire to learn truly and fully what waiting on God is. The lesson is this:
It is with the heart we must wait upon God. "Let your heart take courage."
All our waiting depends upon the state of the heart. As a man's heart is,
so is he before God. We can advance no further or deeper into the holy
place of God's presence to wait on him there, than our heart is prepared
for it by the Holy Spirit. The message is, "Let your heart take courage, all
you that wait on the Lord."

The truth appears so simple that some may ask: "Do not all admit this?
Where is the need of insisting on it so specially?" Because very many
Christians have no sense of the great difference between the religion of the
mind and the religion of the heart, and the former is far more diligently
cultivated than the latter. They know not how infinitely greater the heart
is than the mind. It is in this that one of the chief causes must be sought
of the feebleness of our Christian life, and it is only as this is understood
that waiting on God will bring its full blessing.

Proverbs 3:5 may help to make my meaning plain. Speaking of a life in
the fear and favor of God, it says, "Trust in the Lord with all your heart,
and lean not upon your own understanding." In all religion, we have to
use these two powers. The mind has to gather knowledge from God's

Word, and prepare the food by which the heart with the inner life is to be nourished. But here comes in a terrible danger, of our leaning to our own understanding, and trusting in our understanding of divine things. People imagine that if they are occupied with the truth, the spiritual life will as a matter of course be strengthened. And this is by no means the case. The understanding deals with conceptions and images of divine things, but it cannot reach the real life of the soul. Hence the command, "Trust in the Lord with all your heart, and lean not upon your own understanding." It is with the heart that man believes and comes into touch with God. It is in the heart that God has given his Spirit, to be there to us the presence and the power of God working in us. In all our religion, it is the heart that must trust and love and worship and obey. My mind is utterly impotent in creating or maintaining the spiritual life within me: the heart must wait on God for him to work it in me.

It is in this even as in the physical life. My reason may tell me what to eat and drink, and how the food nourishes me. But in the eating and feeding, my reason can do nothing: the body has its organs for that special purpose. Just so, reason may tell me what God's Word says, but it can do nothing to the feeding of the soul on the bread of life. This the heart alone can do by its faith and trust in God. A man may be studying the nature and effects of food or sleep. When he wants to eat or sleep, he sets aside his thoughts and study, and uses the power of eating or sleeping. And so the Christian needs ever, when he has studied or heard God's Word, to cease from his thoughts, to put no trust in them, and to awaken his heart to open itself before God, and seek the living fellowship with him.

This is now the blessedness of waiting upon God, that I confess the impotence of all my thoughts and efforts, and set myself still to bow my heart before him in holy silence, and to trust him to renew and strengthen his own work in me. And this is just the lesson of our text, "Let your heart take courage, all you that wait on the Lord." Remember the difference between knowing with the mind and believing with the heart. Beware of the temptation of leaning upon your understanding with its clear, strong thoughts. They only help you to know what the heart must get from God; in themselves they are but images and shadows. "Let your heart take cour-age, all you that wait on the Lord." Present it before him as that wonderf part of your spiritual nature in which God reveals himself, and by w¹ you can know him. Cultivate the greatest confidence that, thoug' cannot see into your heart, God is working there by his Holy Sr the heart wait at times in perfect silence and quiet; in its hidden depths God will work. Be sure of this, and just wait on him.

No knowledge of the air or the food around me can nourish me, except it enter into my inward life. And no knowledge of the truths of God can profit me, except as he, by his Spirit, enters into my inmost being and dwells within me. It is with the heart I must wait upon God; it is into the heart I must receive God; it is in the heart, God will give his Spirit and every spiritual blessing in Christ. Give your whole heart, with its secret workings, into God's hands continually. He wants the heart, and takes it, and, as God, dwells in it. "Be strong, and let your heart take courage, all you that wait on the Lord."

My soul, wait only upon God!

In Humble Fear and Hope

Behold, the eye of the Lord is upon them that fear him,
upon them that hope in his mercy, to deliver their soul
from death, and to keep them alive in famine. Our soul has
waited for the Lord; he is our help and our shield.
For our heart shall rejoice in him, because we have trusted
in his holy name. Let Your mercy, O Lord, be upon us,
according as we wait for you.
—*Psalm 33:18–22*

God's eye is upon his people; their eye is upon him. In waiting upon God, our eye, looking up to him, meets his looking down upon us. This is the blessedness of waiting upon God: that it takes our eyes and thoughts away from ourselves, even our needs and desires, and occupies us with our God. We worship him in his glory and love, with his all-seeing eye watching over us, that he may supply our every need. Let us consider this wonderful meeting between God and his people, and mark well what we are taught here of those on whom God's eye rests, and of him on whom our eye rests.

"The eye of the Lord is on them that fear him, on them that hope in his mercy." Fear and hope are generally thought to be in conflict with each other; in the presence and worship of God, they are found side by side in perfect and beautiful harmony. And this because in God himself, all apparent contradictions are reconciled. Righteousness and peace, judgment and mercy, holiness and love, infinite power and infinite gentleness, a majesty that is exalted above all heaven, and a condescension that bows very low, meet and kiss each other. There is, indeed, a fear that has torment, that is cast out entirely by perfect love. But there is a fear that is found in the very heavens. In the song of Moses and the Lamb they sing, "Who shall not fear you, O Lord, and glorify your name?" And out of the very throne the voice came, "Praise our God, all his servants, and you that fear him." Let us in our waiting ever seek "to fear the glorious and fearful name, the Lord your God." The deeper we bow before his holiness in holy fear and adoring awe, in deep reverence and humble self-abasement, even as the angels veil their faces before the throne, the more will his holiness rest upon us, and the soul be fitted to have God reveal himself; the deeper we enter into the truth "that no flesh glory in his presence," will it be given us to see his glory. "The eye of the Lord is on them that fear him."

"On them that hope in his mercy." So far will the true fear of God be from keeping us back from hope, it will stimulate and strengthen it. The lower we bow, the deeper we feel we have nothing to hope in but his mercy. The lower we bow, the nearer God will come, and make our hearts bold to trust him. Let every exercise of waiting, let our whole habit of waiting on God, be pervaded by abounding hope—a hope as bright and boundless as God's mercy. The fatherly kindness of God is such that, in whatever state we come to him, we may confidently hope in his mercy.

Such are God's waiting ones. And now, think of the God on whom we wait. "The eye of the Lord is on them that fear him, on them that hope in his mercy, to deliver their soul from death, and to keep them alive in famine." Not to prevent the danger of death and famine—this is often needed to stir up to wait on him—but to deliver and to keep alive. The dangers are often very real and dark; the situation, whether in the temporal or spiritual life, may appear to be utterly hopeless; there is always one hope: God's eye is on them. That eye sees the danger, and sees in tender love his trembling, waiting child, and sees the moment when the heart is ripe for the blessing, and sees the way in which it is to come. This living, mighty God—oh, let us fear him and hope in his mercy. And let us humbly but boldly say: "Our soul waits for the Lord; he is our help and our shield. Let your mercy be upon us, O Lord, according as we wait for you."

Oh, the blessedness of waiting on such a God! A very present help in every time of trouble; a shield and defense against every danger. Children of God! Will you not learn to sink down in entire helplessness and impotence, and in stillness to wait and see the salvation of God? In the utmost spiritual famine, and when death appears to prevail—oh, wait on God! He does deliver; he does keep alive. Say it not only in solitude, but say it to each other. The psalm speaks not of one, but of God's people— "Our soul waits on the Lord: he is our help and our shield." Strengthen and encourage each other in the holy exercise of waiting, that each may not only say it of himself, but of his brethren, "We have waited for him; we will be glad and rejoice in his salvation."

My soul, wait only upon God!

DAY 11

Patiently

Rest in the Lord, and wait patiently for him. Those that wait
upon the Lord, they shall inherit the land.
—*Psalm 37:7–9*

"In patience possess your souls." "You have need of patience." "Let patience
have its perfect work, that you may be perfect and entire." Such words
of the Holy Spirit show us what an important element in the Christian
life and character patience is. And nowhere is there a better place for
cultivating or displaying it than in waiting on God. There we discover
how impatient we are, and what our impatience means. We confess at
times that we are impatient with men and circumstances that hinder us,
or with ourselves and our slow progress in the Christian life. If we truly
set ourselves to wait upon God, we shall find that it is with him we are
impatient, because he does not at once, or as soon as we could wish,
do our bidding. It is in waiting upon God that our eyes are opened to
believe in his wise and sovereign will, and to see that the sooner and the
more completely we yield absolutely to it, the more surely his blessing
can come to us.

"It is not of him that wills, nor of him that runs, but of God that shows
mercy." We have as little power to increase or strengthen our spiritual life,
as we had to originate it. We were born not of the will of the flesh, nor of
the will of man, but of the will of God. Even so, our willing and running,
our desire and effort, avail nought; all is "of God that shows mercy." All
the exercises of the spiritual life, our reading and praying, our willing
and doing, have their very great value. But they can go no farther than

this, that they point the way and prepare us in humility to look to and to depend alone upon God himself, and in patience to await his good time and mercy. The waiting is to teach us our absolute dependence upon God's mighty working, and to make us in perfect patience place ourselves at his disposal. They that wait on the Lord shall inherit the land; the promised land and its blessing. The heirs must wait; they can afford to wait.

"Rest in the lord, and wait patiently for him." It is resting in the Lord, in his will, his promise, his faithfulness, and his love, that makes patience easy. And the resting in him is nothing but being silent unto him, still before him. Having our thoughts and wishes, our fears and hopes, hushed into calm and quiet in that great peace of God which passes all understanding. That peace keeps the heart and mind when we are anxious for anything, because we have made our request known to him. The rest, the silence, the stillness, and the patient waiting, all find their strength and joy in God himself.

The need and the reasonableness and the blessedness of patience will be opened up to the waiting soul. Our patience will be seen to be the counterpart of God's patience. He longs far more to bless us fully than we can desire it. But, as the husbandman has long patience until the fruit be ripe, so God bows himself to our slowness and bears long with us. Let us remember this, and wait patiently: of each promise and every answer to prayer, the word is true, "I, the Lord, will hasten it in its time."

"Rest in the Lord, and wait patiently for him." Yes, for him. Seek not only the help, the gift you need; seek himself; wait for him. Give God his glory by resting in him, by trusting him fully, by waiting patiently for him. This patience honors him greatly; it leaves him, as God on the throne, to do his work; it yields self wholly into his hands. It lets God be God. If your waiting be for some special request, wait patiently. If your waiting be more the exercise of the spiritual life seeking to know and have more of God, wait patiently. Whether it be in the shorter specific periods of waiting, or as the continuous habit of the soul; rest in the Lord, be still before the Lord, and wait patiently. "They that wait on the Lord shall inherit the land."

My soul, wait only upon God!

DAY 12

Keeping his Ways

Wait on the Lord, and keep his way,
and he shall exalt you to inherit the land.
—*Psalm 37:34*

If we desire to find a man whom we long to meet, we inquire where the places and the ways are where he is to be found. When waiting on God, we need to be very careful that we keep his ways; out of these, we never can expect to find him. "You meet him that rejoices and works righteousness; those that remember you in your ways." We may be sure that God is never and nowhere to be found but in his ways. And that there, by the soul who seeks and patiently waits, he is always most surely to be found. "Wait on the Lord, and keep his ways, and he shall exalt you."

How close the connection between the two parts of the injunction. "Wait on the Lord"—that has to do with worship and disposition—"and keep his ways"—that deals with walk and work. The outer life must be in harmony with the inner; the inner must be the inspiration and the strength for the outer. It is our God who has made known his ways in his Word for our conduct, and invites our confidence for his grace and help in our heart. If we do not keep his ways, our waiting on him can bring no blessing. The surrender to a full obedience to all his will is the secret of full access to all the blessings of his fellowship.

Notice how strongly this comes out in the psalm. It speaks of the evil-doer who prospers in his way, and calls on the believer not to fret himself. When we see men around us prosperous and happy while they forsake God's ways, and ourselves left in difficulty or suffering, we are in danger of first fretting at what appears so strange, and then gradually yielding to seek our prosperity in their path. The psalm says: "Fret not yourself; trust in the Lord, and do good. Rest in the Lord, and wait patiently for him; cease from anger, and forsake wrath. Depart from evil, and do good; the Lord forsakes not his saints. The righteous shall inherit the land. The law of his God is in his heart; none of his steps shall slide." And then follows—the word occurs for the third time in the psalm—"Wait on the Lord, and keep his ways." Do what God asks you to do; God will do more than you can ask him to do.

And let no one give way to the fear, "I cannot keep his ways." It is this robs us of our confidence. It is true, you have not the strength yet to keep all his ways. But keep carefully those for which you have received strength already. Surrender yourself willingly and trustingly to keep all God's ways, in the strength which will come in waiting on him. Give up your whole being to God without reserve and without doubt; he will prove himself God to you, and work in you that which is pleasing in his sight through Jesus Christ. Keep his ways, as you know them in the Word. Keep his ways, as nature teaches them, in always doing what appears right. Keep his ways, as Providence points them out. Keep his ways, as the Holy Spirit suggests. Do not think of waiting on God while you say you are not willing to walk in his path. However weak you feel, only be willing, and he who has worked to will, will work to do by his power.

"Wait on the Lord, and keep his ways." It may be that the consciousness of shortcoming and sin makes our text look more like a hindrance than a help in waiting on God. Let it not be so. Have we not said more than once, the very starting point and groundwork of this waiting is utter and absolute impotence? Why then not come with everything evil you feel in yourself, every memory of unwillingness, unwatchfulness, unfaithfulness, and all that causes such unceasing self-condemnation? Put your trust in God's omnipotence, and find in waiting on God your deliverance. Your failure has been owing to only one thing: you sought to conquer and obey in your own strength. Come and bow before God until you learn that he is the God who alone is good, and alone can work any good thing. Believe that in you, and all that nature can do, there is no true power. Be content to receive from God each moment the inworking of his mighty grace and life, and waiting on God will become the renewal of your strength to run in his ways and not be weary, to walk in his paths and never faint. "Wait on the Lord, and keep his ways" will be command and promise in one.

My soul, wait only upon God!

DAY 13

For More than We Know

And now, Lord, what do I wait for? My hope is in you.
Deliver me from all my transgressions.
Psalm 39:7–8

There may be times when we feel as if we knew not what we are waiting for. There may be other times when we think we do know, and when it would just be so good for us to realize that we do not know what to ask as we ought. God is able to do for us exceeding abundantly above what we ask or think, and we are in danger of limiting him when we confine our desires and prayers to our own thoughts of them. It is a great thing at times to say, as our psalm says, "And now, Lord, what wait I for, I scarce know or can tell; this only I can say: 'My hope is in you.'"

How we see this limiting of God in the case of Israel! When Moses promised them meat in the wilderness, they doubted, saying: "Can God furnish a table in the wilderness? He smote the rock that the water gushed out; can he give bread also? Can he provide flesh for his people?" If they had been asked whether God could provide streams in the desert, they would have answered, "Yes." God had done it: he could do it again. But when the thought came of God doing something new, they limited him; their expectation could not rise beyond their past experience or their own thoughts of what was possible. Even so, we may be limiting God by our conceptions of what he has promised or is able to do. Do let us beware of limiting the Holy One of Israel in our very prayer. Let us believe that every promise of God we plead has a divine meaning, infinitely beyond our thoughts of them. Let us believe that his fulfilment of them can be, in a power and an abundance of grace, beyond our largest grasp of thought. And let us therefore cultivate the habit of waiting on God, not only for what we think we need, but for all his grace and power are ready to do for us.

In every true prayer, there are two hearts in exercise. The one is your heart, with its little, dark, human thoughts of what you need and God can do. The other is God's great heart, with its infinite, its divine purposes of blessing. What think you? To which of these two ought the larger place to be given in your approach to him? Undoubtedly, to the heart of God: everything depends upon knowing and being occupied with that. But how little this is done. This is what waiting on God is meant to teach you. Just think of God's wonderful love and redemption, in the meaning these words must have to him. Confess how little you understand what God is willing to do for you, and say each time as you pray, "And now, what do I wait for?" My heart cannot say. God's heart knows and waits to give. "My hope is in you." Wait on God to do for you more than you can ask or think.

Apply this to the prayer that follows: "Deliver me from all my transgressions." You have prayed to be delivered from temper, or pride, or self-will. It is as if it is in vain. May it not be that you have had your own thoughts about the way or the extent of God's doing it, and have never waited on the God of glory, according to the riches of his glory, to do for you what has not entered the heart of man to conceive? Learn to worship God as the God who does wonders, who wishes to prove in you that he can do something supernatural and divine. Bow before him, wait upon him, until your soul realizes that you are in the hands of a divine and almighty worker. Consent not to know what and how he will work; expect it to be something altogether Godlike, something to be waited for in deep humility, and received only by his divine power. Let "And now, Lord, what do I wait for? My hope is in you" become the spirit of every longing and every prayer. He will in his time do his work.

Dear soul, in waiting on God you may often be ready to be weary, because you hardly know what you have to expect. I pray you, be of good courage: this ignorance is often one of the best signs. He is teaching you to leave all in his hands, and to wait on him alone. "Wait on the Lord! Be strong, and let your heart take courage. Yes, wait on the Lord."

My soul, wait only upon God.

DAY 14

The Way to the New Song

> I waited patiently for the Lord, and he inclined unto me,
> and heard my cry. . . . And he has put a new song
> in my mouth, even praise unto our God.
> —*Psalm 40:1–3*

Come and listen to the testimony of one who can speak from experience of the sure and blessed outcome of patient waiting upon God. True patience is so foreign to our self-confident nature; it is so indispensable in our waiting upon God; it is such an essential element of true faith that we may well once again meditate on what the word has to teach us.

The word "patience" is derived from the Latin word for suffering. It suggests the thought of being under the constraint of some power from which we want to be free. At first we submit against our will; experience teaches us that when it is vain to resist, patient endurance is our wisest course. In waiting on God it is of infinite consequence that we not only submit because we are compelled to, but because we lovingly and joyfully consent to be in the hands of our blessed Father. Patience then becomes our highest blessedness and our highest grace. It honors God, and gives him time to have his way with us. It is the highest expression of our faith in his goodness and faithfulness. It brings the soul perfect rest in the assurance that God is carrying on his work. It is the token of our full consent that God should deal with us in such a way and time as he thinks best. True patience is the losing of our self-will in his perfect will.

Such patience is needed for the true and full waiting on God. Such patience is the growth and fruit of our first lessons in the school of waiting. To many a one it will appear strange how difficult it is truly to wait upon God. The great stillness of soul before God that sinks into its own helplessness and waits for him to reveal himself; the deep humility that is afraid to let its own will or its own strength work aught except as God works to will and to do; the meekness that is content to be and to know nothing except as God gives his light; the entire resignation of the will that only wants to be a vessel in which his holy will can move and mold: all these elements of perfect patience are not found at once. But they will come in measure as the soul maintains its position, and ever again says: "Truly, my soul waits upon God; from him comes my salvation: he only is my rock and my salvation."

Have you ever noticed what proof we have that patience is a grace for which very special grace is given, in these words of Paul: "Strengthened with all might, according to his glorious power, unto all"—what?— "Patience and long-suffering with joyfulness." Yes, we need to be strengthened with all God's might, and that according to the measure of his glorious power, if we are to wait on God in all patience. It is God revealing himself in us as our life and strength that will enable us with perfect patience to leave all in his hands. If any are inclined to despond because they have not such patience, let them be of good courage; it is in the course of our feeble and very imperfect waiting that God himself by his hidden power strengthens us and works out in us the patience of the saints, the patience of Christ himself.

Listen to the voice of one who was deeply tried: "I waited patiently for the Lord, and he inclined unto me, and heard my cry." Hear what he passed through: "He brought me up also out of an horrible pit, out of the miry clay, and set my feet upon a rock, and established my goings. And he has put a new song in my mouth, even praise unto our God." Patient waiting upon God brings a rich reward; the deliverance is sure; God himself will put a new song into your mouth. O soul! Be not impatient, whether it be in the exercise of prayer and worship that you find it difficult to wait, or in the delay in respect of definite requests, or in the fulfilling of your heart's desire for the revelation of God himself in a deeper spiritual life—fear not, but rest in the Lord, and wait patiently for him. And if you sometimes feel as if patience is not your gift, then remember it is God's gift, and take that prayer, "The Lord direct your hearts into the patience of Christ" (2 Thessalonians 3:5). Into the patience with which you are to wait on God, he himself will guide you.

My soul, wait only upon God!

DAY 15

For His Counsel

They soon forgot his works; they waited not for his counsel;
. . . they provoked him with their counsel.
—*Psalm 106:13, 43*

This is said of the sin of God's people in the wilderness. He had wonderfully redeemed them, and was prepared as wonderfully to supply their every need. But, when the time of need came, "They waited not for his counsel." They thought not that the Almighty God was their Leader and Provider; they asked not what his plans might be. They simply thought the thoughts of their own heart, and tempted and provoked God by their unbelief. "They waited not for his counsel."

How this has been the sin of God's people in all ages! In the land of Canaan, in the days of Joshua, the only three failures of which we read were owing to this one sin. In going up against Ai, in making a covenant with the Gibeonites, in settling down without going up to possess the whole land, they waited not for his counsel. And so even the advanced believer is in danger from this most subtle of temptations: taking God's Word and thinking his own thoughts of them, and not waiting for his counsel. Let us take the warning and see what Israel teaches us. And let us very specially regard it not only as a danger to which the individual is exposed, but as one against which God's people, in their collective capacity, need to be on their guard.

Our whole relation to God is rooted in this: that his will is to be done in us and by us as it is in heaven. He has promised to make known his will to us by his Spirit, the Guide into all truth. And our position is to be that of waiting for his counsel, as the only guide of our thoughts and actions. In our church worship, in our prayer meetings, in our conventions, in all our gatherings as managers, or directors, or committees, or helpers in any part of the work for God, our first object ought ever to be to ascertain the mind of God. God always works according to the counsel of his will; the more that counsel of his will is sought and found and honored, the more surely and mightily will God do his work for us and through us.

The great danger in all such assemblies is that in our consciousness of having our Bible, and our past experience of God's leading, and our sound creed, and our honest wish to do God's will, we trust in these, and do not realize that with every step we need and may have a heavenly guidance. There may be elements of God's will, applications of God's word, experiences of the close presence and leading of God, manifestations of the power of his Spirit, of which we know nothing as yet. God may be willing—no, God *is* willing—to open up these to the souls who are intently set upon allowing him to have his way entirely, and who are willing in patience to wait for his making it known. When we come together praising God for all he has done and taught and given, we may at the same time be limiting him by not expecting greater things. It was when God had given the water out of the rock that they did not trust him for bread. It was when God had given Jericho into his hands that Joshua thought the victory over Ai was sure; he now knew what God could do, and waited not for counsel from God. And so, while we think that we know and trust the power of God for what we may expect, we may be hindering him by not giving time, and not definitely cultivating the habit of waiting for his counsel.

A minister has no more solemn duty than teaching people to wait upon God. Why was it that in the house of Cornelius, when "Peter spoke these words, the Holy Spirit fell upon all that heard him"? They had said, "We are here before God to hear all things that are commanded you of God." We may come together to give and to listen to the most earnest exposition of God's truth with little spiritual profit if there be not the waiting for God's counsel. In all our gatherings we need to believe in the Holy Spirit as the Guide and Teacher of God's saints when they wait to be led by him into the things which God has prepared, and which the heart cannot conceive.

More stillness of soul to realize God's presence; more consciousness of ignorance of what God's great plans may be; more faith in the certainty that God has greater things to show us; more longing that he himself may be revealed in new glory: these must be the marks of the assemblies of God's saints, if they would avoid the reproach, "They waited not for his counsel."

My soul, wait only upon God!

For His Light in the Heart

I wait for the Lord, my soul does wait, and in his word
do I hope. My soul waits for the Lord more than they that
watch for the morning; I say, more than they
that watch for the morning.
—*Psalm 130:5–6*

With what intense longing the morning light is often waited for. By the mariners in a shipwrecked vessel; by a benighted traveler in a dangerous country; by an army that finds itself surrounded by an enemy. The morning light will show what hope of escape there may be. The morning may bring life and liberty. And so the saints of God in darkness have longed for the light of his countenance, more than watchmen for the morning. They have said, "More than watchmen for the morning, my soul waits for the Lord." Can we say that too? Our waiting on God can have no higher object than simply having his light shine on us, and in us, and through us, all the day.

God is Light. God is a Sun. Paul says, "God has shined in our hearts to give the light." What light? "The light of the glory of God, in the face of Jesus Christ." Just as the sun shines its beautiful, life-giving light on and into our earth, so God shines into our hearts the light of his glory, of his love, in Christ his Son. Our heart is meant to have that light filling and gladdening it all the day. It can have it, because God is our sun, and it is written, "Your sun shall no more go down forever." God's love shines on us without ceasing.

But can we indeed enjoy it all the day? We can. And how can we? Let nature give us the answer. Those beautiful trees and flowers, with all this green grass, what do they do to keep the sun shining on them? They do nothing; they simply bask in the sunshine when it comes. The sun is millions of miles away, but over all that distance it sends its own light and joy; and the tiniest flower that lifts its little head upwards is met by the same exuberance of light and blessing as flood the widest landscape. We have not to care for the light we need for our day's work; the sun cares, and provides and shines the light around us all the day. We simply count upon it, and receive it, and enjoy it.

The only difference between nature and grace is this: that what the trees and the flowers do unconsciously, as they drink in the blessing of the light, is to be with us a voluntary and a loving acceptance. Faith, simple faith in God's word and love, is to be the opening of the eyes, the opening of the heart, to receive and enjoy the unspeakable glory of his grace. And even as the trees, day by day, and month by month, stand and grow into beauty and fruitfulness, just welcoming whatever sunshine the sun may give, so it is the very highest exercise of our Christian life just to abide in the light of God, and let it, and let him, fill us with the life and the brightness it brings.

And if you ask, "But can it really be, that even as naturally and heartily as I recognize and rejoice in the beauty of a bright sunny morning, I can rejoice in God's light all the day?" It can, indeed. From my breakfast table I look out on a beautiful valley, with trees and vineyards and mountains. In our spring and autumn months the light in the morning is exquisite, and almost involuntarily we say, "How beautiful!" And the question comes: "Is it only the light of the sun that is to bring such continual beauty and joy? And is there no provision for the light of God being just as much an unceasing source of joy and gladness?" There is, indeed, if the soul will but be still and wait on him, will only let God shine.

Dear soul! Learn to wait on the Lord, more than watchers for the morning. All within you may be very dark; is that not the very best reason for waiting for the light of God? The first beginnings of light may be just enough to discover the darkness, and painfully to humble you on account of sin. Can you not trust the light to expel the darkness? Do believe it will. Just bow, even now, in stillness before God, and wait on him to shine into you. Say, in humble faith: "God is light, infinitely brighter and more beautiful than that of the sun. God is light. The Father, the eternal, inaccessible, and incomprehensible light. The Son, the light concentrated, and embodied, and manifested. The Spirit, the light entering and dwelling and shining in our hearts. God is light, and is here shining on my heart. I have been so occupied with the rushlights of my thoughts and efforts, I have never opened the shutters to let his light in. Unbelief has kept it out. I bow in faith; God's light is shining into my heart. The God of whom Paul wrote, 'God has shined into our heart,' is my God. What would I think of a sun that could not shine? What shall I think of a God that does not shine? No, God shines! God is light! I will take time, and just be still, and rest in the light of God. My eyes are feeble, and the windows are not clean, but I will wait on the Lord. The light does shine, the light will shine in me, and make me full of light. And I shall learn to walk all the day in the light and joy of God. My soul waits on the Lord, more than watchers for the morning."

My soul, wait only upon God!

DAY 17

In Times of Darkness

I will wait upon the Lord, that hides his face
from the house of Jacob; and I will look for him.
—*Isaiah 8:17*

Here we have a servant of God, waiting upon him, not on behalf of himself, but of his people, from whom God was hiding his face. It suggests to
us how our waiting upon God, though it commences with our personal
needs, with the desire for the revelation of himself, or of the answer to
personal petitions, need not—may not—stop there. We may be walking
in the full light of God's countenance, and God yet be hiding his face
from his people around us; far from our being content to think that this is
nothing but the just punishment of their sin, or the consequence of their
indifference, we are called with tender hearts to think of their sad estate,
and to wait on God on their behalf. The privilege of waiting upon God is
one that brings great responsibility. Even as Christ, when he entered God's
presence, at once used his place of privilege and honor as intercessor, so
we, no less, if we know what it is really to enter in and wait upon God,
must use our access for our less favored brethren. "I will wait upon the
Lord, who hides his face from the house of Jacob."

You worship with a certain congregation. Possibly there is not the
spiritual life or joy either in the preaching or in the fellowship that you
could desire. You belong to a Church, with its many congregations. There
is so much of error or worldliness, of seeking after human wisdom and
culture, of trust in ordinances and observances, that you do not wonder
that God hides his face, in many cases, and that there is but little power

for conversion or true edification. Then there are branches of Christian work with which you are connected—a Sunday school, a gospel hall, a young men's association, a mission work abroad—in which the feebleness of the Spirit's working appears to indicate that God is hiding his face. You think, too, you know the reason. There is too much trust in men and money; there is too much formality and self-indulgence; there is too little faith and prayer; too little love and humility; too little of the spirit of the crucified Jesus. At times you feel as if things are hopeless; nothing will help.

Do believe that God can help and will help. Let the spirit of the prophet come into you, as you take his words, and set yourself to wait on God, on behalf of his erring children. Instead of the tone of judgment or condemnation, of despondency or despair, realize your calling to wait upon God. If others fail in doing it, give yourself doubly to it. The deeper the darkness, the greater the need of appealing to the one and only Deliverer. The greater the self-confidence around you that knows not that it is poor and wretched and blind, the more urgent the call on you who profess to see the evil and to have access to him who alone can help, to be at your post, waiting upon God. As often as you are tempted to complain, or to sigh, say ever afresh: "I will wait on the Lord, who hides his face from the house of Jacob."

There is a still larger circle: the Christian Church throughout the world. Think of Greek, Roman Catholic, and Protestant churches, and the state of the millions that belong to them. Or think only of the Protestant churches with their open Bible and orthodox creeds. How much nominal profession and formality! How much of the rule of the flesh and of man in the very temple of God! And what abundant proof that God does hide his face!

What are those to do who see and mourn this? The first thing to be done is this: "I will wait on the Lord, who hides his face from the house of Jacob." Let us wait on God, in the humble confession of the sins of his people. Let us take time and wait on him in this exercise. Let us wait on God in tender, loving intercession for all saints, our beloved brethren, however wrong their lives or their teaching may appear. Let us wait on God in faith and expectation, until he shows us that he will hear. Let us wait on God, with the simple offering of ourselves to himself, and the earnest prayer that he would send us to our brethren. Let us wait on God, and give him no rest until he make Zion a joy in the earth. Yes, let us rest in the Lord, and wait patiently for him who now hides his face from so many of his children. And let us say of the lifting up of the light of his countenance we desire for all his people, "I wait for the Lord; my soul waits; and my hope is in his word. My soul waits for the Lord, more than the watchers for the morning, the watchers for the morning."

My soul, wait only upon God!

DAY 18

To Reveal Himself
•

And it shall be said in that day, Lo, this is our God; we have
waited for him, and he will save us: this is the Lord; we have
waited for him; we will rejoice and be glad in his salvation.
—*Isaiah 25:9*

In this passage we have two precious thoughts: the one, that it is the language of God's people who have been unitedly waiting on him; the other, that the fruit of their waiting has been that God has so revealed himself, that they could joyfully say, "Lo, this is our God: this is the Lord." The power and the blessing of united waiting is what we need to learn.

Note the twice-repeated "We have waited for him." In some time of trouble, the hearts of the people had been drawn together and they had, ceasing from all human hope or help, with one heart, set themselves to wait for their God. Is not this just what we need in our churches and conventions and prayer meetings? Is not the need of the Church and the world great enough to demand it? Are there not in the Church of Christ evils to which no human wisdom is equal? Have we not ritualism and rationalism, formalism and worldliness, robbing the Church of its power? Have we not culture and money and pleasure threatening its spiritual life? Are not the powers of the Church utterly inadequate to cope with the powers of infidelity and iniquity and wretchedness in Christian countries and in heathendom? And is there not in the promise of God, and in the power of the Holy Spirit, a provision made that can meet the need, and give the Church the restful assurance that she is doing all her God expects of her? And would not united waiting upon God for the supply of his Spirit most certainly seem the needed blessing? We cannot doubt it.

The object of a more definite waiting upon God in our gatherings would be very much the same as in personal worship. It would mean a deeper conviction that God must and will do all; a more humble and abiding entrance into our deep helplessness, and the need of entire and unceasing dependence upon him; a more living consciousness that the essential thing is, giving God his place of honor and of power; a confident expectation that to those who wait on him, God will, by his Spirit, give the secret of his acceptance and presence, and then, in due time, the revelation of his saving power. The great aim would be to bring everyone in a praying and worshiping company under a deep sense of God's presence, so that when they part there will be the consciousness of having met God himself, of having left every request with him, and of now waiting in stillness while he works out his salvation.

It is this experience that is indicated in our text. The fulfillment of the words may, at times, be in such striking interpositions of God's power that all can join in the cry, "Lo, this is our God; this is the Lord!" They may equally become true in spiritual experience, when God's people in their waiting times become so conscious of his presence that in holy awe souls feel, "Lo, this is our God; this is the Lord!"

It is this, alas, that is too much missed in our meetings for worship. The Godly minister has no more difficult, no more solemn, no more blessed task, than to lead his people out to meet God, and, before ever he preaches, to bring each one into contact with him. "We are now here in the presence of God"—these words of Cornelius show the way in which Peter's audience was prepared for the coming of the Holy Spirit. Waiting before God, and waiting for God, and waiting on God, are the one condition of God showing his presence.

A company of believers gathered with the one purpose, helping each other by little intervals of silence, to wait on God alone, opening the heart for whatever God may have of new discoveries of evil, of his will, of new openings in work or methods of work, would soon have reason to say, "Lo, this is our God; we have waited for him, he shall save us; this is the Lord; we have waited for him, we will be glad and rejoice in his salvation."

My soul, wait only upon God!

DAY 19

As a God of Judgment

Yea, in the way of your judgments, O Lord, have we waited
for you. . . . for when your judgments are on the earth,
the inhabitants of the world learn righteousness.
—*Isaiah 26:8–9*

The Lord is a God of judgment: blessed are all they
that wait for him.
—*Isaiah 30:18*

God is a God of mercy and a God of judgment. Mercy and judgment
are ever together in his dealings. In the flood, in the deliverance of Israel
out of Egypt, in the overthrow of the Canaanites, we ever see mercy in
the midst of judgment. Within the inner circle of his own people, we see
it too: the judgment punishes the sin, while mercy saves the sinner. Or,
rather, mercy saves the sinner, not in spite of, but by means of, the very
judgment that came upon his sin. In waiting on God, we must beware of
forgetting this: as we wait, we must expect him as a God of judgment.

"In the way of your judgments, have we waited for you." That will prove
true in our inner experience. If we are honest in our longing for holiness,
in our prayer to be wholly the Lord's, his holy presence will stir up and
discover hidden sin, and bring us very low in the bitter conviction of the
evil of our nature, its opposition to God's law, its impotence to fulfill that
law. The words will come true, "Who may abide the day of his coming,
for he is like a refiner's fire." "Oh, that you would come down, as when
the melting fire burns!" In great mercy God executes within the soul his

judgments upon sin, as he makes it feel its wickedness and guilt. Many a one tries to flee from these judgments: the soul that longs for God, and for deliverance from sin, bows under them in humility and in hope. In silence of soul it says: "Arise, O Lord! And let your enemies be scattered. In the way of your judgments, we have waited for you."

Let no one who seeks to learn the blessed art of waiting on God wonder if at first the attempt to wait on him only discovers more of his sin and darkness. Let no one despair because unconquered sins, or evil thoughts, or great darkness appear to hide God's face. Was not, in his own Beloved Son, the gift and bearer of his mercy on Calvary, the mercy as if hidden and lost in the judgment? Oh, submit, and sink down deep under the judgment of your every sin: judgment prepares the way, and breaks out in wonderful mercy. It is written, "Zion shall be redeemed with judgment." Wait on God, in the faith that his tender mercy is working out in you his redemption in the midst of judgment; wait for him, he will be gracious to you.

There is another application still, one of unspeakable solemnity. We are expecting God, in the way of his judgments, to visit this earth; we are waiting for him. What a thought! We know of these coming judgments; we know that there are tens of thousands of our professing Christians who live on in carelessness, and who, if no change come, must perish under God's hand. Oh, shall we not do our utmost to warn them, to plead with and for them, if God may have mercy on them. If we feel our want of boldness, want of zeal, want of power, shall we not begin to wait on God more definitely and persistently as a God of judgment, asking him so to reveal himself in the judgments that are coming on our very friends, that we may be inspired with a new fear of him and them, and constrained to speak and pray as never yet. Verily, waiting on God is not meant to be a spiritual self-indulgence. Its object is to let God and his holiness, Christ and the love that died on Calvary, the Spirit and fire that burns in heaven and came to earth, get possession of us, to warn and rouse men with the message that we are waiting for God in the way of his judgments. O Christian! Prove that you really believe in the God of judgment.

My soul, wait only upon God!

DAY 20

Who Waits on Us

And therefore will the Lord wait, that he may be gracious
unto you; and therefore will he be exalted, that he may have
mercy upon you: for the Lord is a God of judgment:
blessed are all they that wait for him.
—*Isaiah 30:18*

We must not only think of our waiting upon God, but also of what is more wonderful still, of God's waiting upon us. The vision of him waiting on us will give new impulse and inspiration to our waiting upon him. It will give an unspeakable confidence that our waiting cannot be in vain. If he waits for us, then we may be sure that we are more than welcome; that he rejoices to find those he has been seeking for. Let us seek even now, at this moment, in the spirit of lowly waiting on God, to find out something of what it means, "Therefore will the Lord wait, that he may be gracious unto you." We shall accept and echo back the message: "Blessed are all they that wait for him."

Look up and see the great God upon his throne. He is Love—an unceasing and inexpressible desire to communicate his own goodness and blessedness to all his creatures. He longs and delights to bless. He has inconceivably glorious purposes concerning every one of his children, by the power of his Holy Spirit, to reveal in them his love and power. He waits with all the longings of a father's heart. He waits that he may be gracious unto you. And each time you come to wait upon him, or seek to maintain in daily life the holy habit of waiting, you may look up and see him ready to meet you, waiting that he may be gracious unto you. Yes, connect every exercise, every breath of the life of waiting, with faith's vision of your God waiting for you.

And if you ask, how is it, if he waits to be gracious, that even after I come and wait upon him, he does not give the help I seek, but waits on longer and longer—there is a double answer. The one is this: God is a wise husbandman, "who waits for the precious fruit of the earth, and has long patience for it." He cannot gather the fruit until it is ripe. He knows when we are spiritually ready to receive the blessing to our profit and his glory. Waiting in the sunshine of his love is what will ripen the soul for his blessing. Waiting under the cloud of trial, that breaks in showers of blessing, is as needful. Be assured that if God waits longer than you could wish, it is only to make the blessing doubly precious. God waited four thousand years, until the fullness of time, before he sent his Son. Our times are in his hands; he will avenge his elect speedily; he will make haste for our help, and not delay one hour too long.

The other answer points to what has been said before. The giver is more than the gift; God is more than the blessing; and our being kept waiting on him is the only way for our learning to find our life and joy in himself. Oh, if God's children only knew what a glorious God they have, and what a privilege it is to be linked in fellowship with himself, then they would rejoice in him, even when he keeps them waiting. They would learn to understand better than ever, "Therefore will the Lord wait, that he may be gracious unto you." His waiting will be the highest proof of his graciousness.

"Blessed are all they that wait for him." Our queen has her ladies-in-waiting. The position is one of subordination and service, and yet it is considered one of the highest dignity and privilege because a wise and gracious sovereign makes them companions and friends. What a dignity and blessedness to be attendants-in-waiting on the Everlasting God, ever on the watch for every indication of his will or favor, ever conscious of his nearness, his goodness, and his grace! "The Lord is good to them that wait for him." "Blessed are all they that wait for him." Yes, it is blessed when a waiting soul and a waiting God meet each other. God cannot do his work without his and our waiting his time: let waiting be our work, as it is his. And if his waiting be nothing but goodness and graciousness, let ours be nothing but a rejoicing in that goodness, and a confident expectancy of that grace. And let every thought of waiting become to us simply the expression of unmingled and unutterable blessedness, because it brings us to a God who waits that he may make himself known to us perfectly as the Gracious One.

My soul, wait only upon God!

DAY 21

The Almighty One

They that wait on the Lord shall renew their strength;
they shall mount up with eagle wings; they shall run and
not be weary; they shall walk and not faint.
—*Isaiah 40:31*

Waiting always partakes of the character of our thoughts of the one on whom we wait. Our waiting on God will depend greatly on our faith of what he is. In our text we have the close of a passage in which God reveals himself as the Everlasting and Almighty One. It is as that revelation enters our soul that the waiting will become the spontaneous expression of what we know him to be: a God altogether most worthy to be waited upon.

Listen to the words, "Why say you, O Jacob, my way is hid from the Lord?" Why do you speak as if God does not hear or help?

"Have you not known, have you not heard, that the Everlasting One, the Lord, the Creator of the ends of the earth, faints not, neither is weary?" So far from it, "He gives power to the faint, and to them that have no might he increases strength." Even the youths—"the glory of young men is their strength"—"even the youths shall faint, and the young men shall utterly fall"—all that is accounted strong with man shall come to nought. "But they that wait on the Lord"—on the Everlasting One, who does not faint, neither is weary—they "shall renew their strength; they shall mount up with wings as eagles; they shall run and"—listen now—they shall be strong with the strength of God, and, even as he, "shall not be weary; they shall walk and," even as he, "not faint."

Yes, "They shall mount up with wings as eagles." You know what eagles' wings mean. The eagle is the king of birds; it soars the highest into the heavens. Believers are to live a heavenly life, in the very Presence and Love and Joy of God. They are to live where God lives; they need God's strength to rise there. To them that wait on him it shall be given.

You know how the eagles' wings are obtained. Only in one way—by the eagle birth. You are born of God. You have the eagles' wings. You may not have known it; you may not have used them; but God can and will teach you to use them.

You know how the eagles are taught the use of their wings. See yonder cliff rising a thousand feet out of the sea. See high up a ledge on the rock, where there is an eagle's nest with its treasure of two young eaglets. See the mother bird come and stir up her nest, and with her beak push the timid birds over the precipice. See how they flutter and fall and sink toward the depth. See now "how she flutters over her young, spreads abroad her wings, takes them, bears them on her wings" (Deuteronomy 32:11), and so, as they ride upon her wings, brings them to a place of safety. And so she does once and again, each time casting them out over the precipice, and then again taking and carrying them. "So the Lord alone did lead him." Yes, the instinct of that eagle mother was God's gift, a single ray of that love in which the Almighty trains his people to mount as on eagles' wings.

He stirs up your nest. He disappoints your hopes. He brings down your confidence. He makes you fear and tremble, as all your strength fails, and you feel utterly weary and helpless. And all the while he is spreading his strong wings for you to rest your weakness on, and offering his everlasting Creator-strength to work in you. And all he asks is that you should sink down in your weariness and wait on him, and allow him in his Jehovah-strength to carry you as you ride upon the wings of his Omnipotence.

Dear child of God! I pray you, lift up your eyes, and behold your God! Listen to him who says that he faints not, neither is weary, who promises that you too shall not faint or be weary, who asks nought but this one thing, that you should wait on him. Oh, will you not do what God asks, just be quiet and let him work And let your answer be: With such a God, so mighty, so faithful, so tender—

My soul, wait only upon God!

DAY 22

Its Certainty of Blessing

You shall know that I am the Lord; for they shall
not be ashamed that wait for me.
—*Isaiah 49:23*

Blessed are all they that wait for him.
—*Isaiah 30:18*

What promises! How God seeks to draw us to waiting on him by the
most positive assurance that it never can be in vain: "They shall not be
ashamed that wait for me." How strange that, though we should so often
have experienced it, we are yet so slow of learning that this blessed waiting must and can be as the very breath of our life, a continuous resting in
God's presence and his love, an unceasing yielding of ourselves for him
to perfect his work in us. Let us once again listen and meditate, until our
heart says with new conviction: "Blessed are they that wait for him!" Our
sixth day's lesson we found in the prayer of Psalm 25: "Let none that wait
on you be ashamed." The very prayer shows how we fear lest it might be.
Let us listen to God's answer, until every fear is banished, and we send
back to heaven the words God speaks: Yes, Lord, we believe what you
say, "All they that wait for me shall not be ashamed." "Blessed are all they
that wait for him."

The context of each of these two passages points us to times when
God's Church was in great straits, and to human eye there was no possibility of deliverance. But God interposes with his word of promise, and
pledges his Almighty Power for the deliverance of his people. And it is

as the God who has himself undertaken the work of their redemption, that he invites them to wait on him, and assures them that disappointment is impossible. We, too, are living in days in which there is much in the state of the Church, with its profession and its formalism, that is indescribably sad. Amid all we praise God for, there is, alas, much to mourn over! Were it not for God's promises we might well despair. But in his promises, the Living God has given and bound himself to us. He calls us to wait on him. He assures us we shall not be put to shame. Oh, that our hearts might learn to wait before him, until he himself reveals to us what his promises mean, and in the promises reveals himself in his hidden glory! We shall be irresistibly drawn to wait on him alone. God increase the company of those who say, "Our soul waits for the Lord: he is our Help and our Shield."

This waiting upon God on behalf of his Church and people will depend greatly upon the place that waiting on him has taken in our personal life. The mind may often have beautiful visions of what God has promised to do, and the lips may speak of them in stirring words, but these are not really the measure of our faith or power. No; it is what we really know of God in our personal experience, conquering the enemies within, reigning and ruling, revealing himself in his Holiness and Power in our inmost being—it is this that will be the real measure of the spiritual blessing we expect from him, and bring to our fellow men. It is as we know how blessed the waiting on God has become to our own souls, that we shall confidently hope in the blessing to come on the Church around us, and the key-word of all our expectations will be. He has said: "All they that wait on me shall not be ashamed." From what he has done in us, we shall trust him to do mighty things around us.

"Blessed are all they that wait for him." Yes, blessed even now in the waiting. The promised blessings, for ourselves, or for others, may tarry; the unutterable blessedness of knowing and having him who has promised, the Divine Blesser, the Living Fountain of the coming blessings, is even now ours. Do let this truth get full possession of your souls, that waiting on God is itself the highest privilege of the creature, the highest blessedness of his redeemed child.

Even as the sunshine enters with its light and warmth, with its beauty and blessing, into every little blade of grass that rises upward out of the cold earth, so the Everlasting God meets, in the greatness and the tenderness of his love, each waiting child, to shine in his heart "the light of the knowledge of the glory of God in the face of Jesus Christ." Read these words again, until your heart learns to know what God waits to do to you. Who can measure the difference between the great sun and that little blade of grass? And yet the grass has all of the sun it can need or hold. Do believe that in waiting on God, his greatness and your littleness suit and meet each other most wonderfully. Just how in emptiness and poverty and utter impotence, in humility and meekness and surrender to his will, before his great glory, and be still. As you wait on him, God draws near. He will reveal himself as the God who will fulfill mightily his every promise. And let your heart ever again take up the song, "Blessed are all they that wait for him."

My soul, wait only upon God!

DAY 23

For Unlooked-for Things

For since the beginning of the world men have not heard,
nor perceived by the ear, neither has the eye seen, O God,
beside you, what he has prepared for him that waits for him.
—*Isaiah 64:4*

The Revised Version has, "Neither hath the eye seen a God beside thee, which worketh for him that waiteth for him." In the King James Version, the thought is that "no eye hath seen the thing which God hath prepared." In the Revised Version, "no eye hath seen a God, beside our God, who worketh for him that waiteth for him." To both the two thoughts are common: that our place is to wait upon God, and that there will be revealed to us what the human heart cannot conceive. The difference is, in the Revised Version it is the God who works; in the King James Version the thing he is to work. In 1 Corinthians 2:9, the citation is in regard to the things which the Holy Spirit is to reveal, as in the King James Version, and in this meditation we keep to that.

The previous verses, specially from Isaiah 63:15, refer to the low state of God's people. The prayer has been poured out, "Look down from heaven" (Isaiah 63:15). "Why have you hardened my heart from your fear? Return for your servants' sake" (Isaiah 63:19). And Isaiah 64:1, still more urgent: "Oh, that you would rend the heavens, that you would come down . . . as when the melting fire burns, to make your name known to your adversaries!" Then follows the plea from the past: "When you did terrible things we looked not for, you came down, the mountains flowed down at your presence." "For"—this is now the faith that has been awakened by the thought of things we looked not for, he is still the same God—"eye has not seen beside you, O God, what he has prepared for him that waits for him." God alone knows what he can do for his waiting people. As Paul expounds and applies it, "The things of God knows no man, save the Spirit of God." "But God has revealed them to us by his Spirit."

The need of God's people, and the call for God's interposition, is as urgent in our days as it was in the time of Isaiah. There is now, as there was then, as there has been at all times, a remnant that seek after God with their whole heart. But if we look at Christendom as a whole, at the state of the Church of Christ, there is infinite cause for beseeching God to rend the heavens and come down. Nothing but a special interposition of Almighty Power will avail. I fear we have no right conception of what the so-called Christian world is in the sight of God. Unless God comes down "as the melting fire burns, to make known his name to his adversaries," our labors are comparatively fruitless. Look at the ministry—how much it is in the wisdom of man and of literary culture—how little in demonstration of the Spirit and of power. Think of the unity of the body—how little there is of the manifestation of the power of a heavenly love binding God's children into one. Think of holiness—the holiness of Christ-like humility and crucifixion to the world—how little the world sees that they have men among them who live in Christ in heaven, in whom Christ and heaven live.

What is to be done? There is but one thing. We must wait upon God. And what for? We must cry, with a cry that never rests, "Oh, that you would rend the heavens and come down, that the mountains might flow down at your presence." We must desire and believe, we must ask and expect, that God will do unlooked-for things. We must set our faith on a God of whom men do not know what he has prepared for them that wait for him. The wonder-doing God, who can surpass all our expectations, must be the God of our confidence.

Yes, let God's people enlarge their hearts to wait on a God able to do exceeding abundantly above what we can ask or think. Let us band ourselves together as his elect who cry day and night to him for things men have not seen. He is able to arise and to make his people a name, and a praise in the earth. "He will wait, that he may be gracious unto you; blessed are all they that wait for him."

My soul, wait only upon God!

DAY 24

To Know his Goodness

The Lord is good unto them that wait for him.
—*Lamentations 3:25*

"There is none good but God." "His goodness is in the heavens." "Oh, how great is your goodness, which you have laid up for them that fear you." "Oh, taste and see that the Lord is good!" And here is now the true way of entering into and rejoicing in this goodness of God—waiting upon him. The Lord is good—even his children often do not know it, for they wait not in quietness for him to reveal it. But to those who persevere in waiting, whose souls do wait, it will come true. One might think that it is just those who have to wait who might doubt it. But this is only when they do not wait, but grow impatient. The truly waiting ones will all have to say, "The Lord is good to them that wait for him." If you would fully know the goodness of God, give yourself more than ever to a life of waiting on him.

At our first entrance into the school of waiting upon God, the heart is chiefly set upon the blessings which we wait for. God graciously uses our need and desire for help to educate us for something higher than we were thinking of. We were seeking gifts; he, the Giver, longs to give himself and to satisfy the soul with his goodness. It is just for this reason that he often withholds the gifts, and that the time of waiting is made so long. He is all the time seeking to win the heart of his child for himself. He wishes that we should not only say, when he bestows the gift, "How good is God," but that long before it comes, and even if it never comes, we should all the time be experiencing, "It is good that a man should quietly wait." "The Lord is good to them that wait for him."

What a blessed life the life of waiting then becomes—the continual worship of faith, adoring and trusting his goodness. As the soul learns its secret, every act or exercise of waiting just becomes a quiet entering into the goodness of God, to let it do its blessed work and satisfy our every need. And every experience of God's goodness gives the work of waiting new attractiveness, and, instead of only taking refuge in time of need, there comes a great longing to wait continually and all the day. And however duties and engagements occupy the time and the mind, the soul gets more familiar with the secret art of always waiting. Waiting becomes the habit and disposition, the very second nature and breath of the soul.

Dear Christian! Do you not begin to see that waiting is not one among a number of Christian virtues, to be thought of from time to time, but that it expresses that disposition which lies at the very root of the Christian life? It gives a higher value and a new power to our prayer and worship, to our faith and surrender, because it links us, in unalterable dependence, to God himself. And it gives us the unbroken enjoyment of the goodness of God: "The Lord is good to them that wait for him."

Let me press upon you once again to take time and trouble to cultivate this so much needed element of the Christian life. We get too much of religion at second hand from the teaching of men. That teaching has great value if, even as the preaching of John the Baptist sent his disciples away from himself to the Living Christ, it leads us to God himself. What our religion needs is, more of God. Many of us are too much occupied with our work. As with Martha, the very service we want to render the Master separates from him; it is neither pleasing to him nor profitable to ourselves. The more work, the more need of waiting upon God; the doing of God's will would then, instead of exhausting, be our meat and drink, nourishment and refreshment and strength. "The Lord is good to them that wait for him." How good none can tell but those who prove it in waiting on him. How good none can fully tell but those who have proved him to the utmost.

My soul, wait only upon God!

Quietly

It is good that a man should both hope and
quietly wait for the salvation of the Lord.
—Lamentations 3:26

"Take heed, and be quiet: fear not, neither be faint-hearted." "In quietness
and in confidence shall be your strength." Such words reveal to us the
close connection between quietness and faith, and show us what a deep
need there is of quietness, as an element of true waiting upon God. If we
are to have our whole heart turned towards God, we must have it turned
away from the creature, from all that occupies and interests, whether of
joy or sorrow. God is a being of such infinite greatness and glory, and
our nature has become so estranged from him, that it needs our whole
heart and desires set upon him, even in some little measure to know and
receive him. Everything that is not God, that excites our fears, or stirs
our efforts, or awakens our hopes, or makes us glad, hinders us in our
perfect waiting on him. The message is one of deep meaning: "Take heed
and be quiet." "In quietness shall be your strength." "It is good that a man
should quietly wait."

How the very thought of God in his majesty and holiness should silence
us, Scripture abundantly testifies.

"The Lord is in his holy temple; let all the earth keep silence before
him" (Habakkuk 2:20).

"Hold your peace at the presence of the Lord God" (Zephaniah 1:7).

"Be silent, O all flesh, before the Lord; for he is raised up out of his
holy habitation" (Zechariah 2:13).

As long as the waiting on God is chiefly regarded as an end towards more effectual prayer, and the obtaining of our petitions, this spirit of perfect quietness will not be obtained. But when it is seen that the waiting on God is itself an unspeakable blessedness, one of the highest forms of fellowship with the Holy One, the adoration of him in his glory will of necessity humble the soul into a holy stillness, making way for God to speak and reveal himself. Then it comes to the fulfilment of the precious promise, that all of self and self-effort shall be humbled: "The haughtiness of man shall be brought down, and the Lord alone shall be exalted in that day."

Let everyone who would learn the art of waiting on God remember the lesson: "Take heed, and be quiet," and, "It is good that a man quietly wait." Take time to be separate from all friends and all duties, all cares and all joys; time to be still and quiet before God. Take time not only to secure stillness from man and the world, but from self and its energy. Let the Word and prayer be very precious—but remember, even these may hinder the quiet waiting. The activity of the mind in studying the Word, or giving expression to its thoughts in prayer, the activities of the heart, with its desires and hopes and fears, may so engage us that we do not come to the still waiting on the All-Glorious One; our whole being is not prostrate in silence before him. Though at first it may appear difficult to know how thus quietly to wait, with the activities of mind and heart for a time subdued, every effort after it will be rewarded; we shall find that it grows upon us, and the little season of silent worship will bring a peace and a rest that give a blessing not only in prayer, but all the day.

"It is good that a man should quietly wait for the salvation of the Lord." Yes, it is good. The quietness is the confession of our impotence, that with all our willing and running, with all our thinking and praying, it will not be done: we must receive it from God. It is the confession of our trust that our God will in his time come to our help—the quiet resting in him alone. It is the confession of our desire to sink into our nothingness, and to let him work and reveal himself. Do let us wait quietly. In daily life let there be in the soul that is waiting for the great God to do his wondrous work, a quiet reverence, an abiding watching against too deep engrossment with the world, and the whole character will come to bear the beautiful stamp: Quietly waiting for the salvation of God.

My soul, wait only upon God!

In Holy Expectation

*Therefore will I look to the Lord; I will wait
for the God of my salvation; my God will hear me.*
—*Micah 7:7*

Have you ever read a beautiful little book, *Expectation Corner*? If not, get it; you will find in it one of the best sermons on our text. It tells of a king who prepared a city for some of his poor subjects. Not far from them were large storehouses, where everything they could need was supplied if they but sent in their requests. But on one condition—that they should be on the outlook for the answer, so that when the king's messengers came with the gifts they had desired, they should always be found waiting and ready to receive them. The sad story is told of one desponding one who never expected to get what he asked, because he was too unworthy. One day he was taken to the king's storehouses, and there, to his amazement, he saw, with his address on them, all the packages that had been made up for him, and sent. There was the garment of praise, and the oil of joy, and the eye salve, and so much more; they had been to his door, but found it closed; he was not on the outlook. From that time on he understood the lesson Micah would teach us today: "I will look to the Lord; I will wait for the God of my salvation; my God will hear me."

We have more than once said, waiting for the answer to prayer is not the whole of waiting, but only a part. Today we want to take in the blessed truth, it is a part, and a very important one. When we have special petitions, in connection with which we are waiting on God, our waiting must be very definitely in the confident assurance: "My God will hear me." A holy, joyful expectancy is of the very essence of true waiting. And this not only in reference to the many varied requests every believer has to make, but most especially to the one, great petition which ought to be the chief thing every heart seeks for itself—that the life of God in the soul may have full sway; that Christ may be fully formed within; and that we may be filled to all the fullness of God. This is what God has promised. This is what God's people too little seek, very often because they do not believe it possible. This is what we ought to seek and dare to expect, because God is able and waiting to work it in us.

But God himself must work it. And for this end, our working must cease. We must see how entirely it is to be the faith of the operation of God who raised Jesus from the dead—just as much as the resurrection, the perfecting of God's life in our souls is to be directly his work. And waiting has to become more than ever a tarrying before God in stillness of soul, counting upon him who raises the dead, and calls the things that are not as though they were.

Just notice how the threefold use of the name of God in our text points us to himself as the one from whom alone is our expectation. "I will look to the Lord; I will wait for the God of my salvation; my God will hear me." Everything that is salvation, everything that is good and holy, must be the direct mighty work of God himself within us. For every moment of a life in the will of God, there must be the immediate operation of God. And the one thing I have to do is this: to look to the Lord; to wait for the God of my salvation; to hold fast the confident assurance, "My God will hear me."

God says, "Be still, and know that I am God." There is no stillness like that of the grave. In the grave of Jesus, in the fellowship of his death, in death to self with its own will and wisdom, its own strength and energy, there is rest. As we cease from self, and our soul becomes still to God, God will arise and show himself. "Be still, and know," then you shall know "that I am God." There is no stillness like the stillness Jesus gives when he speaks, "Peace, be still." In Christ, in his death, and in his life, in his perfected redemption, the soul may be still, and God will come in, and take possession, and do his perfect work.

My soul, be still only unto God!

DAY 27

For Redemption

Simeon was just and devout, waiting for the consolation of
Israel, and the Holy Spirit was upon him.
Anna, a prophetess . . . spoke of him to all them
that looked for redemption in Jerusalem.
—*Luke 2:25, 38*

Here we have the mark of a waiting believer. Just, righteous in all his
conduct; devout, devoted to God, ever walking as in his presence; waiting for the consolation of Israel, looking for the fulfillment of God's
promises: and the Holy Spirit was on him. In the devout waiting he had
been prepared for the blessing. And Simeon was not the only one. Anna
spoke to all that looked for redemption in Jerusalem. This was the one
mark, amid surrounding formalism and worldliness, of a Godly band of
men and women in Jerusalem. They were waiting on God—looking for
his promised redemption.

And now that the Consolation of Israel has come, and the redemption
has been accomplished, do we still need to wait? We do indeed. But will
not our waiting, who look back to it as come, differ greatly from those
who looked forward to it as coming? It will, especially in two aspects.
We now wait on God in the full power of the redemption; and we wait
for its full revelation.

Our waiting is now in the full power of the redemption. Christ spoke:
"In that day you shall know that you are in me. Abide in me." The Epistles
teach us to present ourselves to God, "as indeed dead to sin, and alive
to God in Christ Jesus," "blessed with all spiritual blessings in heavenly

places in Christ Jesus." Our waiting on God may now be in the wonderful consciousness, wrought and maintained by the Holy Spirit within us, that we are accepted in the Beloved, that the love that rests on him rests on us, that we are living in that love, in the very nearness and presence and sight of God. The old saints took their stand on the word of God, and waited, hoping on that word; we rest on the word, too—but, oh, under what exceeding greater privileges, as one with Christ Jesus. In our waiting on God, let this be our confidence: in Christ we have access to the Father; how sure, therefore, may we be that our waiting cannot be vain.

Our waiting differs also in this, that while they waited for a redemption to come, we see it accomplished, and now wait for its revelation in us. Christ not only said, "Abide in me," but also "I in you." The Epistles not only speak of us in Christ, but of Christ in us, as the highest mystery of redeeming love. As we maintain our place in Christ day by day, God waits to reveal Christ in us, in such a way that he is formed in us, that his mind and disposition and likeness acquire form and substance in us, so that by each it can in truth be said, "Christ lives in me."

My life in Christ up there in heaven and Christ's life in me down here on earth—these two are the complement of each other. And the more my waiting on God is marked by the living faith, "I in Christ," the more the heart thirsts for and claims the Christ in me. And the waiting on God, which began with special needs and prayer, will increasingly be concentrated, as far as our personal life is concerned, on this one thing: "Lord, reveal your redemption fully in me; let Christ live in me."

Our waiting differs from that of the old saints in the place we take and the expectations we entertain. But at root it is the same: waiting on God, from whom alone is our expectation.

Learn from Simeon and Anna one lesson. How utterly impossible it was for them to do anything towards the great redemption—towards the birth of Christ or his death. It was God's work. They could do nothing but wait. Are we as absolutely helpless as regards the revelation of Christ in us? We are indeed. God did not work out the great redemption in Christ as a whole, and leave its application in detail to us.

The secret thought that it is so lies at the root of all our feebleness. The revelation of Christ in every individual believer, and in each one the daily revelation, step by step and moment by moment, is as much the work of God's omnipotence as the birth or resurrection of Christ. Until this truth enters and fills us, and we feel that we are just as dependent upon

God for each moment of our life in the enjoyment of redemption as they were in their waiting for it, our waiting upon God will not bring its full blessing. The sense of utter and absolute helplessness, the confidence that God can and will do all—these must be the marks of our waiting as of theirs. As gloriously as God proved himself to them the faithful and wonderworking God, he will to us also.

My soul, wait only upon God!

DAY 28

For the Coming of His Son

Be you yourselves like unto men that wait for their Lord.
—*Luke 3:36*

Until the appearing of our Lord Jesus Christ, which in his
own time he shall show, who is the blessed and only
Potentate, the King of kings, and Lord of lords.
—*1 Timothy 6:14–15*

Turned to God from idols to serve the living and true God,
and to wait for his Son from heaven.
—*1 Thessalonians 1:9–10*

Waiting on God in heaven, and waiting for his Son from heaven, these two God has joined together, and no man may put them asunder. The waiting on God for his presence and power in daily life will be the only true preparation for waiting for Christ in humility and true holiness. The waiting for Christ coming from heaven to take us to heaven will give the waiting on God its true tone of hopefulness and joy. The Father, who in his own time will reveal his Son from heaven, is the God who, as we wait on him, prepares us for the revelation of his Son. The present life and the coming glory are inseparably connected in God and in us.

There is sometimes a danger of separating them. It is always easier to be engaged with the religion of the past or the future than to be faithful in the religion of today. As we look to what God has done in the past, or will do in time to come, the personal claim of present duty and present submission to his working may be escaped. Waiting on God must ever lead to waiting for Christ as the glorious consummation of his work; and waiting for Christ must ever remind us of the duty of waiting upon God, as our only proof that the waiting for Christ is in spirit and in truth. There is such a danger of our being so occupied with the things that are coming more than with him who is to come; there is such scope in the study of coming events for imagination and reason and human ingenuity, that nothing but deeply humble waiting on God can save us from mistaking the interest and pleasure of intellectual study for the true love of him and his appearing. All you that say you wait for Christ's coming, be sure that you wait on God now. All you who seek to wait on God now to reveal his Son in you, see to it that you do so as men waiting for the revelation of his Son from heaven. The hope of that glorious appearing will strengthen you in waiting upon God for what he is to do in you now: the same omnipotent love that is to reveal that glory is working in you even now to fit you for it.

"The blessed hope and the appearing of the glory of our great God and Savior Jesus Christ," is one of the great bonds of union given to God's Church throughout the ages. "He shall come to be glorified in his saints, and to be marveled at in all them that believe." Then we shall all meet, and the unity of the body of Christ be seen in its divine glory. It will be the meeting place and the triumph of divine love; Jesus receiving his own and presenting them to the Father; his own meeting him and worshiping in speechless love that blessed face; his own meeting each other in the ecstasy of God's own love. Let us wait, long for, and love the appearing of our Lord and Heavenly Bridegroom. Tender love to him and tender love to each other is the true and only bridal spirit.

I fear greatly that this is sometimes forgotten. A beloved brother in Holland was speaking about the expectancy of faith being the true sign of the bride. I ventured to express a doubt. An unworthy bride, about to be married to a prince, might only be thinking of the position and the riches that she was to receive. The expectancy of faith might be strong, and true love utterly wanting. It is love in the bridal spirit. It is not when we are most occupied with prophetic subjects, but when in humility and love we are clinging close to our Lord and his brethren, that we are in the bride's place. Jesus refuses to accept our love except as it is love to his disciples. Waiting for his coming means waiting for the glorious coming manifestation of the unity of the body, while we seek here to maintain that unity in humility and love. Those who love most are the most ready for his coming. Love to each other is the life and beauty of his bride, the Church.

And how is this to be brought about? Beloved child of God! If you would learn aright to wait for his Son from heaven, live even now waiting on God in heaven. Remember how Jesus lived ever waiting on God. He could do nothing of himself. It was God who perfected his Son through suffering and then exalted him. It is God alone who can give you the deep spiritual life of one who is really waiting for his Son: wait on God for it. Waiting for Christ himself is, oh, so different from waiting for things that may come to pass! The latter any Christian can do; the former, God must work in you every day by his Holy Spirit. Therefore all you who wait on God, look to him for grace to wait for his Son from heaven in the Spirit which is from heaven. And you who would wait for his Son, wait on God continually to reveal Christ in you.

The revelation of Christ in us, as it is given to them who wait upon God, is the true preparation for the full revelation of Christ in glory. It is Christ in us who is the hope of glory.

My soul, wait only upon God!

DAY 29

For the Promise of the Father

He charged them not to depart from Jerusalem,
but to wait for the promise of the Father.
—*Acts 1:4*

In speaking of the saints in Jerusalem at Christ's birth, with Simeon and Anna, we saw how, though the redemption they waited for is come, the call to waiting is no less urgent now than it was then. We wait for the full revelation in us of what came to them, but what they scarce could comprehend. Even so it is with waiting for the promise of the Father. In one sense, the fulfillment can never come again as it came at Pentecost. In another sense, and that in as deep reality as with the first disciples, we daily need to wait for the Father to fulfill his promise in us.

The Holy Spirit is not a person distinct from the Father in the way two persons on earth are distinct. The Father and the Spirit are never without or separate from each other: the Father is always in the Spirit; the Spirit works nothing but as the Father works in him. Each moment the same Spirit that is in us, is in God too, and he who is most full of the Spirit will be the first to wait on God most earnestly, further to fulfill his promise, and still strengthen him mightily by his Spirit in the inner man. The Spirit in us is not a power at our disposal. Nor is the Spirit an independent power, acting apart from the Father and the Son. The Spirit is the real, living presence and the power of the Father working in us, and therefore it is just he who knows that the Spirit is in him, who will wait on the Father for the full revelation and experience of what the Spirit's indwelling is, for his increase and abounding more and more.

We see this in the apostles. They were filled with the Spirit at Pentecost. When they, not long after, on returning from the Council, where they had been forbidden to preach, prayed afresh for boldness to speak in his name, a fresh coming down of the Holy Spirit was the Father's fresh fulfilment of his promise.

At Samaria, by the word and the Spirit, many had been converted, and the whole city filled with joy. At the apostles' prayer the Father once again fulfilled the promise. Even so to the waiting company—"We are all here before God"—in Cornelius' house. And so, too, in Acts 13. It was when men, filled with the Spirit, prayed and fasted, that the promise of the Father was afresh fulfilled, and the leading of the Spirit was given from heaven, "Separate me Barnabas and Saul."

So also we find Paul in Ephesians, praying for those who have been sealed with the Spirit, that God would grant them the spirit of illumination. And later on, that he would grant them, according to the riches of his glory, to be strengthened with might by the Spirit in the inner man.

The Spirit given at Pentecost was not a something that God parted with in heaven, and sent away out of heaven to earth. God does not, cannot, give away anything in that way. When he gives grace, or strength, or life, he gives it by giving himself to work it—it is all inseparable from himself. Much more so is the Holy Spirit. He is God, present and working in us: the true position in which we can count upon that working with an unceasing power is as we, praising for what we have, still unceasingly wait for the Father's promise to be still more mightily fulfilled.

What new meaning and promise does this give to our life of waiting! It teaches us ever to keep the place where the disciples tarried at the footstool of the Throne. It reminds us that, as helpless as they were to meet their enemies, or to preach to Christ's enemies, until they were endued with power, we too can only be strong in the life of faith, or the work of love, as we are in direct communication with God and Christ, and they maintain the life of the Spirit in us. It assures us that the Omnipotent God will, through the glorified Christ, work in us a power that can bring to pass things unexpected, things impossible. Oh, what will not the Church be able to do when her individual members learn to live their lives waiting on God, and when together, with all of self and the world sacrificed in the fire of love, they unite in waiting with one accord for the promise of the Father, once so gloriously fulfilled, but still unexhausted.

Come and let each of us be still in presence of the inconceivable grandeur of this prospect: the Father waiting to fill the Church with the Holy Ghost. "And willing to fill me," let each one say.

With this faith let there come over the soul a hush and a holy fear, as it waits in stillness to take it all in. And let life increasingly become a deep joy in the hope of the ever fuller fulfilment of the Father's promise.

My soul, wait only upon God!

DAY 30

Continually

Therefore turn to your God: keep mercy and judgment,
and wait on your God continually.
—*Hosea 12:6*

Continuity is one of the essential elements of life. Interrupt it for a single hour in a man, and it is lost; he is dead. Continuity, unbroken and ceaseless, is essential to a healthy Christian life. God wants me to be, and God waits to make me; I want to be, and I wait on him to make me, every moment, what he expects of me, and what is well-pleasing in his sight. If waiting on God be of the essence of true religion, the maintenance of the spirit of entire dependence must be continuous. The call of God, "Wait on your God continually," must be accepted and obeyed. There may be times of special waiting; the disposition and habit of soul must be there unchangeably and uninterruptedly.

This waiting continually is indeed a necessity. To those who are content with a feeble Christian life, it appears a luxury something beyond what is essential to being a good Christian. But all who are praying the prayer, "Lord! Make me as holy as a pardoned sinner can be made! Keep me as near to you as it is possible for me to be! Fill me as full of your love as you are willing to do!" feel at once that it is something that must be had. They feel that there can be no unbroken fellowship with God, no full abiding in Christ, no maintaining of victory over sin and readiness for service, without waiting continually on the Lord.

The waiting continually is a possibility. Many think that with the duties of life it is out of the question. They cannot be always thinking of it. Even when they wish to, they forget. They do not understand that it is a matter of the heart, and that what the heart is full of, occupies it, even when the thoughts are otherwise engaged. A father's heart may be filled continuously with intense love and longing for a sick wife or child at a distance, even though pressing business requires all his thoughts. When the heart has learned how entirely powerless it is for one moment to keep itself or bring forth any good, when it has understood how surely and truly God will keep it, when it has, in despair of itself, accepted God's promise to do for it the impossible, it learns to rest in God, and in the midst of occupations and temptations it can wait continually.

This waiting is a promise. God's commands are enablings: gospel precepts are all promises, a revelation of what our God will do for us. When first you begin waiting on God, it is with frequent intermission and frequent failure. But do believe God is watching over you in love and secretly strengthening you in it. There are times when waiting appears to be just losing time, but it is not so. Waiting, even in darkness, is unconscious advance, because it is God you have to do with, and he is working in you. God who calls you to wait on him sees your feeble efforts, and works it in you. Your spiritual life is in no respect your own work; as little as you began it, can you continue it. It is God's Spirit who has begun the work in you of waiting upon God; he will enable you to wait continually.

Waiting continually will be met and rewarded by God himself working continually. We are coming to the end of our meditations. Would that you and I might learn one lesson: God must, God *will*, work continually. He ever does work continually, but the experience of it is hindered by unbelief. But he who by his Spirit teaches you to wait continually will bring you to experience also how, as the Everlasting One, his work is never-ceasing. In the love and the life and the work of God, there can be no break, no interruption.

Do not limit God in this by your thoughts of what may be expected. Do fix your eyes upon this one truth: in his very nature, God, as the only Giver of life, cannot do otherwise than every moment work in his child. Do not look only at the one side: "If I wait continually, God will work continually." No, look at the other side. Place God first and say, "God works continually, every moment I may wait on him continually." Take time until the vision of your God working continually, without one moment's intermission, fill your being. Your waiting continually will then come of itself. Full of trust and joy, the holy habit of the soul will be, "On you do I wait all the day." The Holy Spirit will keep you ever waiting.

My soul, wait only upon God!

Moment by Moment

Words by Daniel W. Whittle, 1893
Music in Christian Endeavor Hymns by Ira D. Sankey

Dying with Jesus, by death reckoned mine,
Living with Jesus a new life divine;
Looking to Jesus till glory doth shine,
Moment by moment, O Lord, I am thine.

Refrain
Moment by moment I'm kept in his love,
Moment by moment I've life from above;
Looking to Jesus till glory doth shine;
Moment by moment, O Lord, I am thine.

Never a battle with wrong for the right,
Never a contest that he doth not fight;
Lifting above us his banner so white,
Moment by moment I'm kept in his sight.

Refrain

Never a trial that he is not there,
Never a burden that he doth not bear,
Never a sorrow that he does not share,
Moment by moment I'm under his care.

Refrain

Never a heartache, and never a groan,
Never a teardrop, and never a moan;
Never a danger but there on the throne
Moment by moment he thinks of his own.

Refrain

Never a weakness that he doth not feel,
Never a sickness that he cannot heal;
Moment by moment, in woo or in weal,
Jesus, my Savior, abides with me still.

Refrain

DAY 31

Only

My soul, wait only upon God; for my expectation
is from him. He only is my rock and my salvation.
—*Psalm 62:5-6*

It is possible to be waiting continually on God, but not only upon him;
there may be other secret confidences intervening and preventing the
blessing that was expected. And so the word "only" must come to throw
its light on the path to the fullness and certainty of blessing. "My soul,
wait only upon God. He only is my rock."

Yes, "My soul, wait only upon God." There is but one God, but one
source of life and happiness for the heart; he only is my rock; my soul, wait
only upon him. You desire to be good. "There is none good but God," and
there is no possible goodness but what is received directly from him. You
have sought to be holy: "There is none holy but the Lord," and there is no
holiness but what he by his Spirit of holiness every moment breathes in
you. You want to live and work for God and his kingdom, for men and
their salvation. Hear how he says, "The Everlasting God, the Creator of the
ends of the earth." He alone "faints not, neither is weary. He gives power
to the faint, and to them that have no might he increases strength. They
that wait upon the Lord shall renew their strength." He only is God; he
only is your rock: "My soul, wait only upon God."

"My soul, wait only upon God." You will not find many who can help
you in this. Enough there will be of your brethren to draw you to put
trust in churches and doctrines, in schemes and plans and human appli-
ances, in means of grace and divine appointments. But, "My soul, wait

only upon God himself." His most sacred appointments become a snare when trusted in. The brazen serpent becomes Nehushtan; the ark and the temple a vain confidence. Let the Living God alone, none and nothing but he, be your hope.

"My soul, wait only upon God." Eyes and hands and feet, mind and thought, may have to be intently engaged in the duties of this life; "My soul, wait only upon God." You are an immortal spirit, created not for this world but for eternity and for God. O my soul! Realize your destiny. Know your privilege, and "wait only upon God." Let not the interest of religious thoughts and exercises deceive you; they very often take the place of waiting upon God. My soul, you must wait, your very self, your inmost being, with all its power, "wait only upon God." God is for you, you are for God; wait only upon him.

Yes, "My soul, wait only upon God." Beware of your two great enemies—the world and self. Beware lest any earthly satisfaction or enjoyment, however innocent it appears, keep you back from saying, "I will go to God, my exceeding joy." Remember and study what Jesus says about denying self, "Let a man deny himself." Gerhard Tersteegen says: "The saints deny themselves in everything." Pleasing self in little things may be strengthening it to assert itself in greater things. "My soul, wait only upon God." Let him be all your salvation and all your desire. Say continually and with an undivided heart, "From him comes my expectation; he only is my rock; I shall not be moved." Whatever be your spiritual or temporal need, whatever the desire or prayer of your heart, whatever your interest in connection with God's work in the Church or the world—in solitude or in the rush of the world, in public worship or other gatherings of the saints, "My soul, wait only upon God." Let your expectations be from him alone. He only is your rock.

"My soul, wait only upon God." Never forget the two foundation-truths on which this blessed waiting rests. If ever you are inclined to think this "waiting only" is too hard or too high, they will recall you at once. They are your absolute helplessness and the absolute sufficiency of your God. Oh, enter deep into the entire sinfulness of all that is of self, and think not of letting self have anything to say one single moment. Enter deep into your utter and unceasing impotence ever to change what is evil in you, or to bring forth anything that is spiritually good. Enter deep into your relation of dependence as creature on God, to receive from him every moment what he gives. Enter deeper still into his covenant of redemption, with his promise to restore more gloriously than ever what you had lost, and by his Son and Spirit to give within you unceasingly, his actual divine Presence and Power. And thus wait upon your God continually and only.

"My soul, wait only upon God." No words can tell, no heart conceive, the riches of the glory of this mystery of the Father and of Christ. Our God, in the infinite tenderness and omnipotence of his love, waits to be our Life and Joy. O my soul! Let it be no longer needed that I repeat the words, "Wait upon God," but let all that is in me rise and sing: "Truly my soul waits upon God. On you do I wait all the day."

My soul, wait only upon God!

Note

My publishers have just issued a work of William Law on the Holy Spirit. In the introduction, I have said how much I owe to the book. I cannot but think that anyone who will take the trouble to read it thoughtfully will find rich spiritual profit in connection with a life of waiting on God.

What he puts more clearly than I have anywhere else found are these cardinal truths:

1. That the very nature and being of God, as the only possessor and dispenser of any life there is in the universe, imply that he must every moment communicate to every creature the power by which it exists, and therefore also much more the power by which it can do that which is good.

2. That the very nature and being of a creature, as owing its existence to God alone, and equally owing to him each moment the continuation of that existence, imply that its happiness can only be found in absolute unceasing momentary dependence upon God.

3. That the great value and blessing of the gift of the Spirit at Pentecost, as the fruit of Christ's redemption, is that it is now possible for God to take possession of his redeemed children and work in them as he did before the fall in Adam. We need to know the Holy Spirit as the presence and power of God in us restored to their true place.

4. That in the spiritual life our great need is the knowledge of two great lessons. The one our entire sinfulness and helplessness—our utter impotence by any effort of our own to do anything towards the maintenance and increase of our inner spiritual life. The other, the infinite willingness of God's love, which is nothing but a desire to communicate himself and his blessedness to us, to meet our every need, and every moment to work in us by his Son and Spirit what we need.

5. That, therefore, the very essence of true religion, whether in heaven or upon earth, consists in an unalterable dependence upon God, because we can give God no other glory, than yielding ourselves to the love which created us to show forth in us its glory, that it may now perfect its work in us.

I need not point out how deep down these truths go to the very root of the spiritual life, and especially the life of waiting on God. I am confident that those who are willing to take the trouble of studying this thoughtful writer will thank me for the introduction to his book.

Absolute Surrender

"I am yours, and all that I have."
—*1 Kings 20:4*

Absolute Surrender

"And Ben-hadad the king of Syria gathered all his host
together: and there were thirty and two kings with him, and
horses, and chariots: and he went up and besieged Samaria,
and warred against it. And he sent messengers to Ahab king of
Israel into the city, and said unto him, Thus says Ben-hadad,
Your silver and your gold are mine; your wives also and your
children, even the goodliest, are mine. And the king of Israel
answered and said, My lord, O king, according to your saying,
I am yours and all that I have."
—*1 Kings 20:1–4*

What Ben-hadad asked was absolute surrender, and what Ahab gave was
what was asked of him: absolute surrender. I want to use these words, "My
lord, O king, according to your saying, I am yours, and all that I have," as
the words of absolute surrender with which every child of God ought to
yield himself to his Father. We have heard it before, but we need to hear
it very definitely: the condition of God's blessing is absolute surrender of
all into his hands. Praise God! If our hearts are willing for that, there is no
end to what God will do for us and to the blessing God will bestow.

"Absolute surrender"—let me tell you where I got those words. I used
them myself often, and you have heard them numberless times. But in
Scotland, once, I was in a company where we were talking about the condition of Christ's Church and what the great need of the Church and of
believers is. And there was in our company a godly worker who has much
to do in training workers, and I asked him what he would say was the
great need of the Church and the message that ought to be preached. He
answered very quietly and simply and determinedly: "Absolute surrender
to God is the one thing."

The words struck me as never before. And that man began to tell how, in the workers with whom he had to deal, he finds that if they are sound on that point, even though they be backward, they are willing to be taught and helped, and they always improve. Whereas others, who are not sound there, very often go back and leave the work. The condition for obtaining God's full blessing is absolute surrender to him.

And now I desire by God's grace to give to you this message—that your God in Heaven answers the prayers which you have offered for blessing on yourselves and for blessing on those around you by this one demand: Are you willing to surrender yourselves absolutely into his hands? What is our answer to be? God knows there are hundreds of hearts who have said it, and there are hundreds more who long to say it but hardly dare to do so. And there are hearts who have said it, but who have yet miserably failed, and who feel themselves condemned because they did not find the secret of the power to live that life. May God have a word for all!

Let me say, first of all, that God claims it from us. Yes, it has its foundation in the very nature of God. God cannot do otherwise. Who is God? He is the Fountain of life, the only Source of existence and power and goodness, and throughout the universe there is nothing good but what God works. God has created the sun and the moon and the stars and the flowers and the trees and the grass. And are they not all absolutely surrendered to God? Do they not allow God to work in them just what he pleases? When God clothes the lily with its beauty, is it not yielded up, surrendered, given over to God as he works in its beauty? And God's redeemed children—oh, can you think that God can work his work if there is only half or a part of them surrendered? God cannot do it. God is life and love and blessing and power and infinite beauty, and God delights to communicate himself to every child who is prepared to receive him. But, ah, this one lack of absolute surrender is just the thing that hinders God. And now he comes, and as God he claims it.

You know in daily life what absolute surrender is. You know that everything has to be given up to its special, definite object and service. I have a pen in my pocket, and that pen is absolutely surrendered to the one work of writing, and that pen must be absolutely surrendered to my hand if I am to write properly with it. If another holds it partly, I cannot write properly. This coat is absolutely given up to me to cover my body. This building is entirely given up to religious services. And now, do you expect that in your immortal being, in the divine nature that you have received by regeneration, God can work his work, every day and every hour, unless you are entirely given up to him? God cannot. The temple of Solomon was absolutely surrendered to God when it was dedicated to him. And every one of us is a temple of God in which God will dwell and work mightily on one condition: absolute surrender to him. God claims it, God is worthy of it, and without it God cannot work his blessed work in us.

God not only claims it, but God will work it himself. I am sure there is many a heart that says, "Ah, but that absolute surrender implies so much!" Someone says: "Oh, I have passed through so much trial and suffering, and there is so much of the self-life still remaining, and I dare not face the entire giving of it up because I know it will cause so much trouble and agony."

Alas, alas—that God's children have such thoughts of him, such cruel thoughts. Oh, I come to you with a message, fearful and anxious one. God does not ask you to give the perfect surrender in your strength or by the power of your will. God is willing to work it in you. Do we not read, "It is God that works in us, both to will and to do of his good pleasure" (Philippians 2:13)? And that is what we should seek for: to go on our faces before God until our hearts learn to believe that the everlasting God himself will come in to turn out what is wrong, to conquer what is evil, and to work what is well-pleasing in his blessed sight. God himself will work it in you.

Look at the men in the Old Testament like Abraham. Do you think it was by accident that God found that man, the father of the faithful and the Friend of God, and that it was Abraham himself, apart from God, who had such faith and such obedience and such devotion? You know it is not so. God raised him up and prepared him as an instrument for his glory.

Did not God say to Pharaoh, "For this cause have I raised you up, for to show in you my power" (Exodus 9:16)?

And if God said that of him, will not God say it far more of every child of his?

Oh, I want to encourage you, and I want you to cast away every fear. Come with that feeble desire, and if there is the fear which says, "Oh, my desire is not strong enough; I am not willing for everything that may come; I do not feel bold enough to say I can conquer everything," I pray you, learn to know and trust your God now. Say, "My God, I am willing that you should make me willing." If there is anything holding you back or any sacrifice you are afraid of making, come to God now, and prove how gracious your God is, and be not afraid that he will command from you what he will not bestow.

God comes and offers to work this absolute surrender in you. All these searchings and hungerings and longings that are in your heart—I tell you, they are the drawings of the divine magnet, Christ Jesus. He lived a life of absolute surrender; he has possession of you; he is living in your heart by his Holy Spirit. You have hindered and hindered him terribly, but he desires to help you to get hold of him entirely. And he comes and draws you now by his message and words. Will you not come and trust God to work in you that absolute surrender to himself? Yes, blessed be God, he can do it, and he *will* do it.

God not only claims it and works it, but God accepts it when we bring it to him. God works it in the secret of our heart; God urges us by the hidden power of his Holy Spirit to come and speak it out, and we have to bring and to yield to him that absolute surrender. But remember, when you come and bring God that absolute surrender, it may, as far as your feelings or your consciousness go, be a thing of great imperfection, and you may doubt and hesitate and say, "Is it absolute?"

But, oh, remember there was once a man to whom Christ had said, "If you can believe, all things are possible to him that believes" (Mark 9:23).

And his heart was afraid, and he cried out, "Lord, I believe; help my unbelief" (Mark 9:24).

That was a faith that triumphed over the Devil, and the evil spirit was cast out. And if you come and say, "Lord, I yield myself in absolute surrender to my God"—even though it be with a trembling heart and with the consciousness, "I do not feel the power; I do not feel the determination; I do not feel the assurance"—it will succeed. Be not afraid, but come just as you are, and even in the midst of your trembling, the power of the Holy Spirit will work.

Have you never yet learned the lesson that the Holy Spirit works with mighty power, while on the human side everything appears feeble? Look at the Lord Jesus Christ in Gethsemane. We read that he, "through the eternal Spirit" (Hebrews 9:14), offered himself a sacrifice unto God. The Almighty Spirit of God was enabling him to do it. And yet what agony and fear and exceeding sorrow came over him, and how he prayed! Externally, you can see no sign of the mighty power of the Spirit, but the Spirit of God was there. And even so, while you are feeble and fighting and trembling, in faith in the hidden work of God's Spirit, do not fear, but yield yourself.

And when you do yield yourself in absolute surrender, let it be in the faith that God does now accept of it. That is the great point, and that is what we so often miss—that believers should be thus occupied with God in this matter of surrender. I pray you, be occupied with God. We want to get help, every one of us, so that in our daily life God shall be clearer to us, God shall have the right place and be "all in all." And if we are to have that through life, let us begin now and look away from ourselves and look up to God. Let each believe: While I, a poor worm on earth and a trembling child of God, full of failure and sin and fear, bow here, and no one knows what passes through my heart, and while I in simplicity say, "O God, I accept your terms; I have pleaded for blessing on myself and others; I have accepted your terms of absolute surrender"—while your heart says that in deep silence, remember there is a God present that takes note of it and writes it down in his book, and there is a God present who at that very moment takes possession of you. You may not feel it, you may not realize it, but God takes possession, if you will trust him.

God not only claims it and works it and accepts it when I bring it, but God maintains it. That is the great difficulty with many. People say: "I have often been stirred at a meeting or at a convention, and I have consecrated myself to God, but it has passed away. I know it may last for a week or for a month, but away it fades, and after a time it is all gone."

But listen! It is because you do not believe what I am now going to tell you and remind you of. When God has begun the work of absolute surrender in you, and when God has accepted your surrender, then God holds himself bound to care for it and to keep it. Will you believe that?

In this matter of surrender there are two: God and I—I a worm; God the everlasting and omnipotent Jehovah. Worm, will you be afraid to trust yourself to this mighty God now? God is willing. Do you not believe that he can keep you continually, day by day, and moment by moment?

> *Moment by moment I'm kept in his love;*
> *Moment by moment I've life from above.*

If God allows the sun to shine upon you moment by moment without intermission, will not God let his life shine upon you every moment? And why have you not experienced it? Because you have not trusted God for it, and you do not surrender yourself absolutely to God in that trust.

A life of absolute surrender has its difficulties—I do not deny that. Yes, it has something far more than difficulties: it is a life that with men is absolutely impossible. But by the grace of God, by the power of God, by the power of the Holy Spirit dwelling in us, it is a life to which we are destined and a life that is possible for us—praise God! Let us believe that God will maintain it.

Some of you have read the words of that aged saint who, on his nine-tieth birthday, told of all God's goodness to him—I mean George Muller. What did he say he believed to be the secret of his happiness and of all the blessing which God had given him? He said he believed there were two reasons. The one was that he had been enabled by grace to maintain a good conscience before God day by day; the other was that he was a lover of God's Word. Ah, yes, a good conscience is complete obedience to God day by day and fellowship with God every day in his Word and prayer—that is a life of absolute surrender.

Such a life has two sides: on the one side, absolute surrender to work what God wants you to do; on the other side, to let God work what he wants to do.

First, to do what God wants you to do.

Give up yourselves absolutely to the will of God. You know something of that will—not enough; far from all. But say absolutely to the Lord God, "By your grace I desire to do your will in everything, every moment of every day." Say, "Lord God, not a word upon my tongue but for your glory, not a movement of my temper but for your glory, not an affection of love or hate in my heart but for your glory, and according to your blessed will."

Someone says, "Do you think that possible?"

I ask, "What has God promised you, and what can God do to fill a vessel absolutely surrendered to him?" Oh, God wants to bless you in a way beyond what you expect. From the beginning, ear has not heard, neither has the eye seen, what God has prepared for them that wait for him (1 Corinthians 2:9). God has prepared unheard-of things, blessings much more wonderful than you can imagine, more mighty than you can conceive. They are divine blessings. Oh, say now: "I give myself absolutely to God, to his will—to do only what God wants."

It is God who will enable you to carry out the surrender.

And, on the other side, come and say: "I give myself absolutely to God, to let him work in me, to will and to do of his good pleasure, as he has promised to do."

Yes, the living God wants to work in his children in a way that we cannot understand but that God's Word has revealed, and he wants to work in us every moment of the day. God is willing to maintain our life. Only let our absolute surrender be one of simple, childlike, and unbounded trust.

This absolute surrender to God will wonderfully bless. What Ahab said to his enemy, King Ben-hadad—"My lord, O king, according to your word I am yours, and all that I have"—shall we not say to our God and loving Father? If we do say it, God's blessing will come upon us. God wants us to be separate from the world; we are called to come out from the world that hates God. Come out for God, and say: "Lord, anything for you." If you say that with prayer, and speak that into God's ear, he will accept it, and he will teach you what it means.

I say again, God will bless you. You have been praying for blessing. But do remember, there must be absolute surrender. At every tea table you see it. Why is tea poured into that cup? Because it is empty and given up for the tea. But put ink or vinegar or wine into it, and will they pour the tea into the vessel? And can God fill you, can God bless you, if you are not absolutely surrendered to him? He cannot. Let us believe God has wonderful blessings for us if we will but stand up for God and say, be it with a trembling will, yet with a believing heart: "O God, I accept your demands. I am yours and all that I have. Absolute surrender is what my soul yields to you by divine grace."

You may not have such strong and clear feelings of deliverances as you would desire to have, but humble yourselves in his sight, and acknowledge that you have grieved the Holy Spirit by your self-will, self-confidence, and self-effort. Bow humbly before him in the confession of that, and ask him to break the heart and to bring you into the dust before him. Then, as you bow before him, just accept God's teaching that in your flesh "there dwells no good thing" (Romans 7:18), and that nothing will help you except another life which must come in. You must deny self once and for all. Denying self must every moment be the power of your life, and then Christ will come in and take possession of you.

When was Peter delivered? When was the change accomplished? The change began with Peter weeping, and the Holy Spirit came down and filled his heart.

God the Father loves to give us the power of the Spirit. We have the Spirit of God dwelling within us. We come to God confessing that and praising God for it, and yet confessing how we have grieved the Spirit. And then we bow our knees to the Father to ask that he would strengthen us with all might by the Spirit in the inner man, and that he would fill us with his mighty power. And as the Spirit reveals Christ to us, Christ comes to live in our hearts forever, and the self-life is cast out.

Let us bow before God in humility, and in that humility confess before him the state of the whole Church. No words can tell the sad state of the Church of Christ on earth. I wish I had words to speak what I sometimes feel about it. Just think of the Christians around you. I do not speak of nominal Christians or of professing Christians, but I speak of hundreds and thousands of honest, earnest Christians who are not living a life in the power of God or to his glory. So little power, so little devotion or consecration to God, so little perception of the truth that a Christian is a man utterly surrendered to God's will! Oh, we want to confess the sins of God's people around us, and to humble ourselves. We are members of that sickly body, and the sickliness of the body will hinder us and break us down unless we come to God and in confession separate ourselves from partnership with worldliness and with coldness toward each other— unless we give up ourselves to be entirely and wholly for God.

How much Christian work is being done in the spirit of the flesh and in the power of self! How much work, day by day, in which human energy—our will and our thoughts about the work—is continually manifested, and in which there is but little of waiting upon God and upon the power of the Holy Spirit! Let us make confession. But as we confess the state of the Church and the feebleness and sinfulness of work for God among us, let us come back to ourselves. Who is there who truly longs to be delivered from the power of the self-life, who truly acknowledges that it is the power of self and the flesh, and who is willing to cast all at the feet of Christ? There is deliverance.

I heard of one who had been an earnest Christian and who spoke about the "cruel" thought of separation and death. But you do not think that, do you? What are we to think of separation and death? This: Death was the path to glory for Christ. For the joy set before him, he endured the cross. The cross was the birthplace of his everlasting glory. Do you love Christ? Do you long to be in Christ, and not like him? Let death be to you the most desirable thing on earth—death to self and fellowship with

Christ. Separation—do you think it a hard thing to be called to be entirely free from the world, and by that separation to be united to God and his love, by separation to become prepared for living and walking with God every day? Surely one ought to say: "Anything to bring me to separation, to death, for a life of full fellowship with God and Christ."

Come and cast this self-life and flesh-life at the feet of Jesus. Then trust him. Do not worry yourselves with trying to understand all about it, but come in the living faith that Christ will come into you with the power of his death and the power of his life. And then the Holy Spirit will bring the whole Christ—Christ crucified and risen and living in glory—into your heart.

The Fruit of the Spirit is Love

I want to look at the fact of a life filled with the Holy Spirit more from the practical side, and to show how this life will show itself in our daily walk and conduct.

Under the Old Testament, you know, the Holy Spirit often came upon men as a divine Spirit of revelation to reveal the mysteries of God, or for power to do the work of God. But he did not then dwell in them. Now, many just want the Old Testament gift of power for work but know very little of the New Testament gift of the indwelling Spirit, animating and renewing the whole life. When God gives the Holy Spirit, his great object is the formation of a holy character. It is a gift of a holy mind and spiritual disposition, and what we need above everything else is to say, "I must have the Holy Spirit sanctifying my whole inner life if I am really to live for God's glory."

You might say that when Christ promised the Spirit to the disciples, he did so that they might have power to be witnesses. True, but then they received the Holy Spirit in such heavenly power and reality that he took possession of their whole being at once and so fitted them as holy men for doing the work with power as they had to do it. Christ spoke of power to the disciples, but it was the Spirit filling their whole being that worked the power.

I wish now to dwell upon the passage found in Galatians 5:22, "The fruit of the Spirit is love."

We read that "love is the fulfilling of the law" (Romans 13:10), and my desire is to speak on love as a fruit of the Spirit with a twofold object. One is that this word may be a searchlight in our hearts and give us a test by which to try all our thoughts about the Holy Spirit and all our experience of the holy life. Let us try ourselves by this word. Has this been our daily habit—to seek the being filled with the Holy Spirit as the Spirit of love? "The fruit of the Spirit is love." Has it been our experience that the more we have of the Holy Spirit, the more loving we become? In claiming the Holy Spirit, we should make this the first object of our expectation. The Holy Spirit comes as a Spirit of love.

Oh, if this were true in the Church of Christ, how different her state would be! May God help us to get hold of this simple, heavenly truth that the fruit of the Spirit is a love which appears in the life, and that just as the Holy Spirit gets real possession of the life, the heart will be filled with real, divine, universal love.

One of the great causes why God cannot bless his Church is the want of love. When the body is divided, there cannot be strength. In the time of their great religious wars, when Holland stood out so nobly against Spain, one of their mottoes was "Unity gives strength." It is only when God's people stand as one body, one before God in the fellowship of love, one toward another in deep affection, one before the world in a love that the world can see—it is only then that they will have power to secure the blessing which they ask of God. Remember that if a vessel that ought to be one whole is cracked into many pieces, it cannot be filled. You can take a potsherd, one part of a vessel, and dip out a little water into that, but if you want the vessel full, the vessel must be whole. That is literally true of Christ's Church, and if there is one thing we must pray for still, it is this: Lord, melt us together into one by the power of the Holy Spirit; let the Holy Spirit, who at Pentecost made them all of one heart and one soul, do his blessed work among us. Praise God, we can love each other in a divine love, for "the fruit of the Spirit is love." Give yourselves up to love, and the Holy Spirit will come; receive the Spirit, and he will teach you to love more.

I

Now, why is it that the fruit of the Spirit is love? Because God is love (1 John 4:8). And what does that mean?

It is the very nature and being of God to delight in communicating himself. God has no selfishness; God keeps nothing to himself. God's nature is to be always giving. In the sun and the moon and the stars, in every flower you see it, in every bird in the air, in every fish in the sea, God communicates life to his creatures. And the angels around his throne, the seraphim and cherubim who are flames of fire—whence have they their glory? It is because God is love, and he imparts to them of his brightness and his blessedness. And we, his redeemed children—God delights to pour his love into us. And why? Because, as I said, God keeps nothing for himself. From eternity, God had his only begotten Son, and the Father gave him all things, and nothing that God had was kept back. "God is love."

One of the old Church Fathers said that we cannot better understand the Trinity than as a revelation of divine love—the Father, the loving One, the Fountain of love; the Son, the beloved one, the Reservoir of love in whom the love was poured out; and the Spirit, the living love that united both and then overflowed into this world. The Spirit of Pentecost, the Spirit of the Father, and the Spirit of the Son is love. And when the Holy Spirit comes to us and to other men and women, will he be less a Spirit of love than he is in God? It cannot be; he cannot change his nature. The Spirit of God is love, and "the fruit of the Spirit is love."

II

Why is that so? That was the one great need of mankind, that was the thing which Christ's redemption came to accomplish: to restore love to this world.

When man sinned, why was it that he sinned? Selfishness triumphed— he sought self instead of God. And just look! Adam at once begins to accuse the woman of having led him astray. Love to God had gone; love to man was lost. Look again: of the first two children of Adam, the one becomes a murderer of his brother.

Does not that teach us that sin had robbed the world of love? Ah, what a proof the history of the world has been of love having been lost! There may have been beautiful examples of love even among the heathen, but only as a little remnant of what was lost. One of the worst things sin did for man was to make him selfish, for selfishness cannot love.

The Lord Jesus Christ came down from Heaven as the Son of God's love. "God so loved the world that he gave his only begotten Son" (John 3:16). God's Son came to show what love is, and he lived a life of love here upon earth in fellowship with his disciples, in compassion over the poor and miserable, in love even to his enemies, and he died the death of love. And when he went to Heaven, whom did he send down? The Spirit of love, to come and banish selfishness and envy and pride, and bring the love of God into the hearts of men. "The fruit of the Spirit is love."

And what was the preparation for the promise of the Holy Spirit? You know that promise as found in the fourteenth chapter of John's Gospel. But remember what precedes in the thirteenth chapter. Before Christ promised the Holy Spirit, he gave a new commandment, and about that new commandment he said wonderful things. One thing was: "Even as I have loved you, so love one another." To them his dying love was to be the only law of their conduct and intercourse with each other. What a message to those fishermen, to those men full of pride and selfishness! "Learn to love each other," said Christ, "as I have loved you." And by the grace of God, they did it. When Pentecost came, they were of one heart and one soul. Christ did it for them.

And now he calls us to dwell and to walk in love. He demands that though a man hate you, still you love him. True love cannot be conquered by anything in Heaven or upon the earth. The more hatred there is, the more love triumphs through it all and shows its true nature. This is the love that Christ commanded his disciples to exercise.

What more did he say? "By this shall all men know that you are my disciples, if you have love one to another" (John 13:35).

You all know what it is to wear a badge. And Christ said to his disciples in effect: "I give you a badge, and that badge is love. That is to be your mark. It is the only thing in Heaven or on earth by which men can know me."

Do we not begin to fear that love has fled from the earth? That if we were to ask the world, "Have you seen us wear the badge of love," the world would say: "No; what we have heard of the Church of Christ is that there is not a place where there is no quarreling and separation." Let us ask God with one heart that we may wear the badge of Jesus' love. God is able to give it.

III

"The fruit of the Spirit is love." Why? Because nothing but love can expel and conquer our selfishness.

Self is the great curse, whether in its relation to God or to our fellow men in general or to fellow Christians, thinking of ourselves and seeking our own. Self is our greatest curse. But, praise God, Christ came to redeem us from self. We sometimes talk about deliverance from the self-life—and thank God for every word that can be said about it to help us—but I am afraid some people think deliverance from the self-life means that now they are going to have no longer any trouble in serving God, and they forget that deliverance from self-life means to be a vessel overflowing with love to everybody all the day.

And there you have the reason why many people pray for the power of the Holy Spirit, and they get something but, oh, so little, because they prayed for power for work and power for blessing, but they have not prayed for power for full deliverance from self. That means not only the righteous self in intercourse with God, but the unloving self in intercourse with men. And there is deliverance. "The fruit of the Spirit is love." I bring you the glorious promise of Christ: that he is able to fill our hearts with love.

A great many of us try hard at times to love. We try to force ourselves to love, and I do not say that is wrong; it is better than nothing. But the end of it is always very sad. "I fail continually," such a one must confess. And what is the reason? The reason is simply this: Because they have never learned to believe and accept the truth that the Holy Spirit can pour God's love into their heart. That blessed text—often it has been limited!— "The love of God is shed abroad in our hearts" (Romans 5:5). It has often been understood in this sense: it means the love of God to me. Oh, what a limitation! That is only the beginning. The love of God is always the love of God in its entirety, in its fullness as an indwelling power, a love of God to me that leaps back to him in love and overflows to my fellow men in love—God's love to me, and my love to God, and my love to my fellow-men. The three are one; you cannot separate them.

Do believe that the love of God can be shed abroad in your heart and mine so that we can love all the day.

"Ah," you say, "how little I have understood that!"

Why is a lamb always gentle? Because that is its nature. Does it cost the lamb any trouble to be gentle? No. Why not? It is so beautiful and gentle. Has a lamb to study to be gentle? No. Why does that come so easy? It is its nature. And a wolf—why does it cost a wolf no trouble to be cruel and to put its fangs into the poor lamb or sheep? Because that is its nature. It has not to summon up its courage; the wolf-nature is there.

And how can I learn to love? Never until the Spirit of God fills my heart with God's love, and I begin to long for God's love in a very different sense from which I have sought it so selfishly as a comfort and a joy and a happiness and a pleasure to myself; never until I begin to learn that "God is love" and to claim it and receive it as an indwelling power for self-sacrifice; never until I begin to see that my glory, my blessedness, is to be like God and like Christ in giving up everything in myself for my fellow men. May God teach us that! Oh, the divine blessedness of the love with which the Holy Spirit can fill our hearts! "The fruit of the Spirit is love."

IV

Once again I ask, Why must this be so? And my answer is, Without this we cannot live the daily life of love.

How often, when we speak about the consecrated life, we have to speak about temper, and some people have sometimes said, "You make too much of temper."

I do not think we can make too much of it. Think for a moment of a clock and of what its hands mean. The hands tell me what is within the clock, and if I see that the hands stand still, or that the hands point wrong, or that the clock is slow or fast, I say that something inside the clock is not working properly. And temper is just like the revelation that the clock gives of what is within. Temper is a proof whether the love of Christ is filling the heart or not. How many there are who find it easier in church or in prayer meeting or in work for the Lord—diligent, earnest work—to be holy and happy than in the daily life with wife and children; easier to be holy and happy outside the home than in it! Where is the love of God? In Christ. God has prepared for us a wonderful redemption in Christ, and he longs to make something supernatural of us. Have we learned to long for it and ask for it and expect it in its fullness?

Then there is the tongue! We sometimes speak of the tongue when we talk of the better life and the restful life, but just think what liberty many Christians give to their tongues. They say, "I have a right to think what I like."

When they speak about each other, when they speak about their neighbors, when they speak about other Christians, how often there are sharp remarks! God keep me from saying anything that would be unloving; God shut my mouth if I am not to speak in tender love. But what I am saying is a fact. How often there are found among Christians who are banded together in work sharp criticism, sharp judgment, hasty opinion, unloving words, secret contempt of each other, secret condemnation of each other! Oh, just as a mother's love covers her children and delights in them and has the tenderest compassion with their foibles or failures, so there ought to be in the heart of every believer a motherly love toward every brother and sister in Christ. Have you aimed at that? Have you sought it? Have you ever pleaded for it? Jesus Christ said, "As I have loved you . . . love one another" (John 13:34). And he did not put that among the other commandments, but he said in effect, "That is a new commandment, the one commandment: Love one another as I have loved you" (John 13:34).

It is in our daily life and conduct that the fruit of the Spirit is love. From that there comes all the graces and virtues in which love is manifested: joy, peace, long-suffering, gentleness, goodness; no sharpness or hardness in your tone, no unkindness or selfishness; meekness before God and man. You see that all these are the gentler virtues. I have often thought as I read those words in Colossians, "Put on therefore as the elect of God, holy and beloved, bowels of mercies, kindness, humbleness of mind, meekness, long-suffering" (Colossians 3:12), that if we had written this, we should have put in the foreground the manly virtues such as zeal, courage, and diligence. But we need to see how the gentler, the most womanly virtues are especially connected with dependence upon the Holy Spirit. These are indeed heavenly graces. They never were found in the heathen world. Christ was needed to come from Heaven to teach us. Your blessedness is long-suffering, meekness, kindness; your glory is humility before God. The fruit of the Spirit that he brought from Heaven out of the heart of the crucified Christ and that he gives in our heart is, first and foremost, love.

You know what John says: "No man has seen God at any time. If we love one another, God dwells in us" (1 John 4:12). That is, I cannot see God, but as a compensation I can see my brother, and if I love him, God dwells in me. Is that really true? That I cannot see God, but I must love my brother, and God will dwell in me? Loving my brother is the way to real fellowship with God. You know what John further says in that most solemn test: "If a man say, I love God, and hates his brother, he is a liar; for he that loves not his brother whom he has seen, how can he love God whom he has not seen?" (1 John 4:20). There is a brother, a most unlovable man. He worries you every time you meet him. He is of the very opposite disposition to yours. You are a careful businessman, and you have to do with him in your business. He is most untidy, unbusinesslike. You say: "I cannot love him."

Oh, friend, you have not learned the lesson that Christ wanted to teach above everything. Let a man be what he will; you are to love him. Love is to be the fruit of the Spirit all the day and every day. Yes, listen! If a man loves not his brother whom he has seen—if you don't love that unlovable man whom you have seen—how can you love God whom you have not seen? You can deceive yourself with beautiful thoughts about loving God. You must prove your love to God by your love to your brother: that is the one standard by which God will judge your love to him. If the love of God is in your heart, you will love your brother. The fruit of the Spirit is love.

And what is the reason that God's Holy Spirit cannot come in power? Is it not possible?

You remember the comparison I used in speaking of the vessel. I can dip a little water into a potsherd, a bit of a vessel, but if a vessel is to be full, it must be unbroken. And the children of God, wherever they come together, to whatever church or mission or society they belong, must love each other intensely, or the Spirit of God cannot do his work. We talk about grieving the Spirit of God by worldliness and ritualism and formality and error and indifference, but I tell you, the one thing above everything that grieves God's Spirit is this lack of love. Let every heart search itself and ask that God may search it.

V

Why are we taught that "the fruit of the Spirit is love"? Because the Spirit of God has come to make our daily life an exhibition of divine power and a revelation of what God can do for his children.

In the second and the fourth chapters of Acts, we read that the disciples were of one heart and of one soul. During the three years they had walked with Christ, they never had been in that spirit. All Christ's teaching could not make them of one heart and one soul. But the Holy Spirit came from Heaven and shed the love of God in their hearts, and they were of one heart and one soul. The same Holy Spirit that brought the love of Heaven into their hearts must fill us, too. Nothing less will do. Even as Christ did, one might preach love for three years with the tongue of an angel, but that would not teach any man to love unless the power of the Holy Spirit should come upon him to bring the love of Heaven into his heart.

Think of the church at large. What divisions! Think of the different bodies. Take the question of holiness, take the question of the cleansing blood, take the question of the baptism of the Spirit—what differences are caused among dear believers by such questions! That there are differences of opinion does not trouble me. We do not have the same constitution and temperament and mind. But how often hate, bitterness, contempt, separation, unlovingness are caused by the holiest truths of God's Word! Our doctrines, our creeds, have been more important than love. We often think we are valiant for the truth, and we forget God's command to speak the truth in love. And it was so in the time of the Reformation between the Lutheran and Calvinistic churches. What bitterness there was then in regard to the Holy Supper, which was meant to be the bond of union among all believers! And so, down the ages, the very dearest truths of God have become mountains that have separated us.

If we want to pray in power, and if we want to expect the Holy Spirit to come down in power, and if we want indeed that God shall pour out his Spirit, we must enter into a covenant with God that we love one another with a heavenly love.

Are you ready for that? Only that is true love that is large enough to take in all God's children, the most unloving and unlovable and unworthy and unbearable and trying. If my vow—absolute surrender to God—was true, then it must mean absolute surrender to the divine love to fill me: to be a servant of love to love every child of God around me. "The fruit of the Spirit is love."

Oh, God did something wonderful when he gave Christ at his right hand the Holy Spirit to come down out of the heart of the Father and his everlasting love. And how we have degraded the Holy Spirit into a mere power by which we have to do our work! God forgive us! Oh, that the Holy Spirit might be held in honor as a power to fill us with the very life and nature of God and of Christ!

VI

"The fruit of the Spirit is love." I ask once again, Why is it so? And the answer comes: That is the only power in which Christians really can do their work.

Yes, it is that we need. We want not only love that is to bind us to each other, but we want a divine love in our work for the lost around us. Oh, do we not often undertake a great deal of work, just as men undertake work of philanthropy, from a natural spirit of compassion for our fellow men? Do we not often undertake Christian work because our minister or friend calls us to it? And do we not often perform Christian work with a certain zeal but without having had a baptism of love?

People often ask, "What is the baptism of fire?"

I have answered more than once: I know no fire like the fire of God, the fire of everlasting love that consumed the sacrifice on Calvary. The baptism of love is what the Church needs, and to get that we must begin at once to get down upon our faces before God in confession and plead: "Lord, let love from Heaven flow down into my heart. I am giving up my life to pray and live as one who has given himself up for the everlasting love to dwell in and fill him."

Ah, yes, if the love of God were in our hearts, what a difference it would make! There are hundreds of believers who say: "I work for Christ, and I feel I could work much harder, but I have not the gift. I do not know how or where to begin. I do not know what I can do."

Brother, sister, ask God to baptize you with the Spirit of love, and love will find its way. Love is a fire that will burn through every difficulty. You may be a shy, hesitating man or woman who cannot speak well, but love can burn through everything. God fill us with love! We need it for our work.

You have read many a touching story of love expressed, and you have said, "How beautiful!" I heard one not long ago. A lady had been asked to speak at a rescue home where there were a number of poor women. As she arrived there and got to the window with the matron, she saw outside a wretched object sitting and asked, "Who is that?"

The matron answered: "She has been into the house thirty or forty times, and she has always gone away again. Nothing can be done with her, she is so low and hard."

But the lady said, "She must come in."

The matron then said: "We have been waiting for you, and the company is assembled, and you have only an hour for the address."

The lady replied, "No, this is of more importance," and she went outside where the woman was sitting and said, "My sister, what is the matter?"

"I am not your sister," was the reply.

Then the lady laid her hand on her, and said, "Yes, I am your sister, and I love you." And so she spoke until the heart of the poor woman was touched.

The conversation lasted some time, and the company were waiting patiently. Ultimately the lady brought the woman into the room. There was the poor wretched, degraded creature, full of shame. She would not sit on a chair but sat down on a stool beside the speaker's seat, and she let her lean against her, with her arms around the poor woman's neck, while she spoke to the assembled people. And that love touched the woman's heart; she had found one who really loved her, and that love gave access to the love of Jesus.

Praise God! There is love upon earth in the hearts of God's children, but oh, that there were more!

O God, baptize our ministers with a tender love—and our missionaries and our Bible-readers and our workers and our young men's and young women's associations. Oh, that God would begin with us now, and baptize us with heavenly love!

VII

Once again: It is only love that can fit us for the work of intercession.

I have said that love must fit us for our work. Do you know what the hardest and the most important work is that has to be done for this sinful world? It is the work of intercession, the work of going to God and taking time to lay hold on him.

A man may be an earnest Christian, an earnest minister, and a man may do good, but alas, how often he has to confess that he knows but little of what it is to tarry with God. May God give us the great gift of an intercessory spirit—a spirit of prayer and supplication! Let me ask you in the name of Jesus not to let a day pass without praying for all saints and for all God's people.

I find there are Christians who think little of that. I find there are prayer unions where they pray for the members and not for all believers. I pray you, take time to pray for the Church of Christ. It is right to pray for the heathen, as I have already said. God help us to pray more for them. It is right to pray for missionaries and for evangelistic work and for the unconverted. But Paul did not tell people to pray for the heathen or the unconverted. Paul told them to pray for believers. Do make this your first prayer every day: "Lord, bless your saints everywhere."

The state of Christ's Church is indescribably low. Plead for God's people that he would visit them; plead for each other; plead for all believers who are trying to work for God. Let love fill your heart. Ask Christ to pour it out afresh into you every day. Try to get it into you by the Holy Spirit of God: I am separated unto the Holy Spirit, and the fruit of the Spirit is love. God help us to understand it.

May God grant that we learn day by day to wait more quietly upon him. Do not wait upon God only for ourselves, or the power to do so will soon be lost, but give ourselves up to the ministry and the love of intercession, and pray more for God's people, for God's people round about us, for the Spirit of love in ourselves and in them, and for the work of God we are connected with. And the answer will surely come, and our waiting upon God will be a source of untold blessing and power. "The fruit of the Spirit is love."

Have you a lack of love to confess before God? Then make confession and say before him, "O Lord, my lack of heart, my lack of love—I confess it." And then, as you cast that lack at his feet, believe that the blood cleanses you, that Jesus comes in his mighty, cleansing, saving power to deliver you, and that he will give his Holy Spirit.

"The fruit of the Spirit is love."

Separated unto the Holy Spirit

"Now there were in the church that was at Antioch certain prophets and teachers; as Barnabas, and Simeon that was called Niger, and Lucius of Cyrene, and Manaen . . . and Saul. As they ministered to the Lord, and fasted, the Holy Spirit said, Separate me Barnabas and Saul for the work whereunto I have called them. And when they had fasted and prayed, and laid their hands on them, they sent them away. So they, being sent forth by the Holy Spirit, departed unto Seleucia."
—*Acts 13:1–4*

In the story of our text we shall find some precious thoughts to guide us as to what God would have of us and what God would do for us. The great lesson of the verses quoted is this: The Holy Spirit is the director of the work of God upon the earth. And what we should do if we are to work rightly for God, and if God is to bless our work, is to see that we stand in a right relation to the Holy Spirit, that we give him every day the place of honor that belongs to him, and that in all our work and (what is more) in all our private inner life, the Holy Spirit shall always have the first place. Let me point out to you some of the precious thoughts our passage suggests.

First of all, we see that God has his own plans with regard to his kingdom.

His church at Antioch had been established. God had certain plans and intentions with regard to Asia and with regard to Europe. He had conceived them; they were his, and he made them known to his servants.

Our great Commander organizes every campaign, and his generals and officers do not always know the great plans. They often receive sealed orders, and they have to wait on him for what he gives them as orders. God in Heaven has wishes and a will in regard to any work that ought to be done and to the way in which it has to be done. Blessed is the man who gets into God's secrets and works under God.

Some years ago, in Wellington, South Africa, where I live, we opened a Mission Institute—what is counted there a fine large building. At our opening services, the principal said something that I have never forgotten. He remarked: "Last year we gathered here to lay the foundation stone, and what was there then to be seen? Nothing but rubbish and stones and bricks and ruins of an old building that had been pulled down. There we laid the foundation stone, and very few knew what the building was that was to rise. No one knew it perfectly in every detail except one man: the architect. In his mind it was all clear, and as the contractor and the mason and the carpenter came to their work, they took their orders from him, and the humblest laborer had to be obedient to orders, and the structure rose, and this beautiful building has been completed. And just so," he added, "this building that we open today is but laying the foundation of a work of which only God knows what is to become."

But God has his workers and his plans clearly mapped out, and our position is to wait, so that God should communicate to us as much of his will as each time is needful.

We have simply to be faithful in obedience, carrying out his orders. God has a plan for his Church upon earth. But, alas, we too often make our plan, and we think that we know what ought to be done. We ask God first to bless our feeble efforts, instead of absolutely refusing to go unless God goes before us. God has planned for the work and the extension of his kingdom. The Holy Spirit has had that work given in charge to him—"the work whereunto I have called them." May God, therefore, help us all to be afraid of touching "the ark of God" except as we are led by the Holy Spirit.

Then the second thought: God is willing and able to reveal to his servants what his will is.

Yes, blessed be God, communications still come down from Heaven! As we read here what the Holy Spirit said, so the Holy Spirit will still speak to his Church and his people. In these latter days, he has often done it. He has come to individual men, and by his divine teaching he has led them out into fields of labor that others could not at first understand or approve, into ways and methods that did not recommend themselves to the majority. But the Holy Spirit does still in our time teach his people. Thank God, in our foreign missionary societies and in our home missions, and in a thousand forms of work, the guiding of the Holy Spirit is known, but—we are all ready, I think, to confess—too little known. We have not learned enough to wait upon him. And so we should make a solemn declaration before God: "O God, we want to wait more for you to show us your will."

Do not ask God only for power. Many a Christian has his own plan of working, but God must send the power. The man works in his own will, and God must give the grace—the one reason why God often gives so little grace and so little success. But let us all take our place before God and say: "What is done in the will of God, the strength of God will not be withheld from it; what is done in the will of God must have the mighty blessing of God."

And so let our first desire be to have the will of God revealed.

If you ask me, Is it an easy thing to get these communications from Heaven and to understand them? I can give you the answer. It is easy to those who are in right fellowship with Heaven and who understand the art of waiting upon God in prayer.

How often we ask, How can a person know the will of God? And people want, when they are in perplexity, to pray very earnestly that God should answer them at once. But God can only reveal his will to a heart that is humble and tender and empty. God can only reveal his will in perplexities and special difficulties to a heart that has learned to obey and honor him loyally in little things and in daily life.

That brings me to the third thought: Note the disposition to which the Spirit reveals God's will.

What do we read here? There were a number of men ministering to the Lord and fasting, and the Holy Spirit came and spoke to them. Some people understand this passage very much as they would in reference to a missionary committee of our day. We see there is an open field, and we have had our missions in other fields, and we are going to get on to that field. We have virtually settled that, and we pray about it. But the position was a very different one in those former days. I doubt whether any of them thought of Europe, for later on even Paul himself tried to go back into Asia, till the night vision called him by the will of God. Look at those men. God had done wonders. He had extended the Church to Antioch, and he had given rich and large blessing. Now, here were these men ministering to the Lord, serving him with prayer and fasting. What a deep conviction they have: "It must all come direct from Heaven. We are in fellowship with the risen Lord; we must have a close union with him, and somehow he will let us know what he wants." And there they were, empty, ignorant, helpless, glad and joyful, but deeply humbled.

"O Lord," they seem to say, "we are your servants, and in fasting and prayer we wait upon you. What is your will for us?"

Was it not the same with Peter? He was on the housetop, fasting and praying, and little did he think of the vision and the command to go to Caesarea. He was ignorant of what his work might be.

It is in hearts entirely surrendered to the Lord Jesus, in hearts separating themselves from the world, and even from ordinary religious exercises, and giving themselves up in intense prayer to look to their Lord—it is in such hearts that the heavenly will of God will be made manifest.

You know that word fasting occurs a second time (in the third verse): "They fasted and prayed." When you pray, you love to go into your closet, according to the command of Jesus, and shut the door. You shut out business and company and pleasure and anything that can distract, and you want to be alone with God. But in one way even the material world follows you there. You must eat. These men wanted to shut themselves out from the influences of the material and the visible, and they fasted. What they ate was simply enough to supply the wants of nature, and in the intensity of their souls they thought to give expression to their letting go of everything on earth in their fasting before God. Oh, may God give us that intensity of desire, that separation from everything, because we want to wait upon God, that the Holy Spirit may reveal to us God's blessed will.

The fourth thought: What is now the will of God as the Holy Spirit reveals it? It is contained in one phrase, "separation unto the Holy Spirit." That is the keynote of the message from Heaven.

"Separate me Barnabas and Saul for the work whereunto I have called them. The work is mine, and I care for it, and I have chosen these men and called them, and I want you who represent the Church of Christ upon earth to set them apart unto me."

Look at this heavenly message in its twofold aspect. The men were to be set apart to the Holy Spirit, and the Church was to do this separating work. The Holy Spirit could trust these men to do it in a right spirit. There they were abiding in fellowship with the heavenly, and the Holy Spirit could say to them, "Do the work of separating these men." And these were the men the Holy Spirit had prepared, and he could say of them, "Let them be separated unto me."

Here we come to the very root, to the very life of the need of Christian workers. The question is, What is needed that the power of God should rest upon us more mightily, that the blessing of God should be poured out more abundantly among those poor, wretched people and perishing sinners among whom we labor? And the answer from Heaven is, "I want men separated unto the Holy Spirit."

What does that imply? You know that there are two spirits on earth. Christ said, when he spoke about the Holy Spirit, "The world cannot receive him" (John 14:17). Paul said, "We have received not the spirit of the world, but the Spirit that is of God" (1 Corinthians 2:12). That is the great want in every worker—the spirit of the world going out, and the Spirit of God coming in to take possession of the inner life and of the whole being.

I am sure there are workers who often cry to God for the Holy Spirit to come upon them as a Spirit of power for their work, and when they feel that measure of power and get blessing, they thank God for it. But God wants something more and something higher. God wants us to seek for the Holy Spirit as a Spirit of power in our own heart and life, to conquer self and cast out sin, and to work the blessed and beautiful image of Jesus into us.

There is a difference between the power of the Spirit as a gift and the power of the Spirit for the grace of a holy life. A man may often have a measure of the power of the Spirit, but if there is not a large measure of the Spirit as the Spirit of grace and holiness, the defect will be manifest in his work. He may be made the means of conversion, but he never will help people on to a higher standard of spiritual life, and when he passes away, a great deal of his work may pass away, too. But a man who is separated unto the Holy Spirit is a man who is given up to say, "Father, let the Holy Spirit have full dominion over me, in my home, in my temper, in every word of my tongue, in every thought of my heart, in every feeling toward my fellow men; let the Holy Spirit have entire possession."

Is that what has been the longing and the covenant of your heart with your God—to be a man or a woman separated and given up unto the Holy Spirit? I pray you listen to the voice of Heaven. "Separate me," said the Holy Spirit. Yes, separated unto the Holy Spirit. May God grant that the Word may enter into the very depths of our being to search us, and if we discover that we have not come out from the world entirely, if God reveals to us that the self-life, self-will, self-exaltation are there, let us humble ourselves before him.

Man, woman, brother, sister, you are a worker separated unto the Holy Spirit. Is that true? Has that been your longing desire? Has that been your surrender? Has that been what you have expected through faith in the power of our risen and almighty Lord Jesus? If not, here is the call of faith, and here is the key of blessing: separated unto the Holy Spirit. God write the word in our hearts!

I said the Holy Spirit spoke to that church as a church capable of doing that work. The Holy Spirit trusted them. God grant that our churches, our missionary societies, and our workers' unions, that all our directors and councils and committees may be men and women who are fit for the work of separating workers unto the Holy Spirit. We can ask God for that, too.

Then comes my fifth thought, and it is this: This holy partnership with the Holy Spirit in this work becomes a matter of consciousness and of action.

These men, what did they do? They set apart Paul and Barnabas, and then it is written of the two that they, being sent forth by the Holy Spirit, went down to Seleucia. Oh, what fellowship! The Holy Spirit in Heaven doing part of the work, men on earth doing the other part. After the ordination of the men upon earth, it is written in God's inspired Word that they were sent forth by the Holy Spirit.

And see how this partnership calls to new prayer and fasting. They had for a certain time been ministering to the Lord and fasting, perhaps days. And the Holy Spirit speaks, and they have to do the work and to enter into partnership, and at once they come together for more prayer and fasting. That is the spirit in which they obey the command of their Lord. And that teaches us that it is not only in the beginning of our Christian work, but all along, that we need to have our strength in prayer. If there is one thought with regard to the Church of Christ which at times comes to me with overwhelming sorrow; if there is one thought in regard to my own life of which I am ashamed; if there is one thought of which I feel that the Church of Christ has not accepted it and not grasped it; if there is one thought which makes me pray to God, "Oh, teach us by your grace, new things"—it is the wonderful power that prayer is meant to have in the kingdom. We have so little availed ourselves of it.

We have all read the expression of Christian in Bunyan's great work when he found he had the key in his breast that should unlock the dungeon. We have the key that can unlock the dungeon of atheism and of heathendom. But, oh, we are far more occupied with our work than we are with prayer. We believe more in speaking to men than we believe in speaking to God. Learn from these men that the work which the Holy Spirit commands must call us to new fasting and prayer, to new separation from the spirit and the pleasures of the world, to new consecration to God and to his fellowship. Those men gave themselves up to fasting and prayer, and if in all our ordinary Christian work there were more prayer, there would be more blessing in our own inner life. If we felt and proved and testified to the world that our only strength lay in keeping every minute in contact with Christ, every minute allowing God to work in us—if that were our spirit, would not, by the grace of God, our lives be holier? Would not they be more abundantly fruitful?

I hardly know a more solemn warning in God's Word than that which we find in the third chapter of Galatians, where Paul asked, "Having begun in the Spirit, are you now made perfect by the flesh?" (Galatians 3:3).

Do you understand what that means? A terrible danger in Christian work, just as in a Christian life that is begun with much prayer, begun in the Holy Spirit, is that it may be gradually shunted off on to the lines of the flesh. And the word comes, "Having begun in the Spirit, are you now made perfect by the flesh?" In the time of our first perplexity and helplessness we prayed much to God, and God answered and God blessed, and our organization became perfected, and our band of workers became large. But gradually the organization and the work and the rush have so taken possession of us that the power of the Spirit, in which we began when we were a small company, has almost been lost. Oh, I pray you, note it well! It was with new prayer and fasting, with more prayer and fasting, that this company of disciples carried out the command of the Holy Spirit, "My soul, wait only upon God." That is our highest and most important work. The Holy Spirit comes in answer to believing prayer.

You know, when the exalted Jesus had ascended to the throne, for ten days, the footstool of the throne was the place where his waiting disciples cried to him. And that is the law of the kingdom—the King upon the throne, the servants upon the footstool. May God find us there unceasingly!

Then comes the last thought: What a wonderful blessing comes when the Holy Spirit is allowed to lead and to direct the work, and when it is carried on in obedience to him!

You know the story of the mission on which Barnabas and Saul were sent out. You know what power there was with them. The Holy Spirit sent them, and they went on from place to place with large blessing. The Holy Spirit was their leader further on. You recollect how it was by the Spirit that Paul was hindered from going again into Asia and was led away over to Europe. Oh, the blessing that rested upon that little company of men and upon their ministry unto the Lord!

I pray you, let us learn to believe that God has a blessing for us. The Holy Spirit, into whose hands God has put the work, has been called "the executive of the Holy Trinity." The Holy Spirit has not only power, but he has the Spirit of love. He is brooding over this dark world and every sphere of work in it, and he is willing to bless. And why is there not more blessing? There can be but one answer: We have not honored the Holy Spirit as we should have done. Is there one who can say that that is not true? Is not every thoughtful heart ready to cry: "God forgive me that I have not honored the Holy Spirit as I should have done, that I have grieved him, that I have allowed self and the flesh and my own will to work where the Holy Spirit should have been honored! May God forgive me that I have allowed self and the flesh and the will actually to have the place that God wanted the Holy Spirit to have."

Oh, the sin is greater than we know! No wonder that there is so much feebleness and failure in the Church of Christ!

Peter's Repentance

"And the Lord turned, and looked upon Peter. And Peter
remembered the word of the Lord, how he had said unto him,
Before the cock crows, you shall deny me thrice. And Peter
went out, and wept bitterly."
—*Luke 22:61–62*

That was the turning point in the history of Peter. Christ had said to him,
"You cannot follow me now" (John 13:36). Peter was not in a fit state to
follow Christ, because he had not been brought to an end of himself; he
did not know himself, and he therefore could not follow Christ. But when
he went out and wept bitterly, then came the great change. Christ previously said to him, "When you are converted, strengthen your brethren."
Here is the point where Peter was converted from self to Christ.

I thank God for the story of Peter. I do not know a man in the Bible
who gives us greater comfort. When we look at his character, so full of
failures, and at what Christ made him by the power of the Holy Spirit,
there is hope for every one of us. But remember, before Christ could fill
Peter with the Holy Spirit and make a new man of him, he had to go
out and weep bitterly; he had to be humbled. If we want to understand
this, I think there are four points that we must look at. First, let us look
at Peter the devoted disciple of Jesus; next, at Peter as he lived the life
of self; then at Peter in his repentance; and last, at what Christ made of
Peter by the Holy Spirit.

I. Peter the Devoted Disciple of Christ

Christ called Peter to forsake his nets and follow him. Peter did it at once,
and he afterward could say rightly to the Lord, "We have forsaken all and
followed you" (Matthew 19:27).

Peter was a man of absolute surrender; he gave up all to follow Jesus. Peter was also a man of ready obedience. You remember Christ said to him, "Launch out into the deep, and let down the net." Peter the fisherman knew there were no fish there, for they had been toiling all night and had caught nothing, but he said, "At your word I will let down the net" (Luke 5:4–5). He submitted to the word of Jesus. Further, he was a man of great faith. When he saw Christ walking on the sea, he said, "Lord, if it is you, bid me come unto you" (Matthew 14:28). And at the voice of Christ, he stepped out of the boat and walked upon the water.

And Peter was a man of spiritual insight. When Christ asked the disciples, "Whom do you say that I am?" Peter was able to answer, "You are the Christ, the Son of the living God." And Christ said, "Blessed are you, Simon Bar-jona; for flesh and blood has not revealed it unto you, but my Father which is in heaven." And Christ spoke of him as the "rock" man, and of his having the keys of the kingdom. Peter was a splendid man, a devoted disciple of Jesus, and if he were living nowadays, everyone would say that he was an advanced Christian. And yet how much there was wanting in Peter!

II. Peter Living the Life of Self

You recollect that just after Christ had said to him, "Flesh and blood has not revealed it unto you, but my Father which is in heaven," Christ began to speak about his sufferings, and Peter dared to say, "Be it far from you, Lord; this shall not be unto you." Then Christ had to say, "Get behind me, Satan; for you savor not the things that be of God, but those that be of men" (Matthew 16:22–23).

There was Peter in his self-will, trusting his own wisdom, and actually forbidding Christ to go and die. Whence did that come? Peter trusted in himself and his own thoughts about divine things. We see later on, more than once, that among the disciples there was a questioning who should be the greatest, and Peter was one of them, and he thought he had a right to the very first place. He sought his own honor even above the others. It was the life of self strong in Peter. He had left his boats and his nets, but not his old self.

When Christ had spoken to him about his sufferings and said, "Get behind me, Satan," he followed it up by saying: "If any man will come after me, let him deny himself, and take up his cross, and follow me" (Matthew 16:24). No man can follow him unless he do that. Self must be utterly denied. What does that mean? When Peter denied Christ, we read that he said three times: "I do not know the man." In other words: "I have nothing to do with him; he and I are no friends; I deny having any connection with him." Christ told Peter that he must deny self. Self must be ignored and its every claim rejected. That is the root of true discipleship. But Peter did not understand it and could not obey it. And what happened? When the last night came, Christ said to him, "Before the cock crows twice you shall deny me thrice."

But with what self-confidence Peter said: "Though all should forsake you, yet I will not. I am ready to go with you, to prison and to death" (Mark 14:29; Luke 22:33).

Peter meant it honestly, and Peter really intended to do it. But Peter did not know himself. He did not believe he was as bad as Jesus said he was.

We perhaps think of individual sins that come between us and God, but what are we to do with that self-life which is all unclean—our very nature? What are we to do with that flesh that is entirely under the power of sin? Deliverance from that is what we need. Peter knew it not, and therefore it was that in his self-confidence he went forth and denied his Lord.

Notice how Christ uses that word "deny" twice. He said to Peter the first time, "Deny self"; he said to Peter the second time, "You will deny me." It is either of the two. There is no choice for us; we must either deny self or deny Christ. There are two great powers fighting each other—the self-nature in the power of sin, and Christ in the power of God. Either of these must rule within us.

It was self that made the Devil. He was an angel of God, but he wanted to exalt self. He became a Devil in hell. Self was the cause of the fall of man. Eve wanted something for herself, and so our first parents fell into all the wretchedness of sin. We, their children, have inherited an awful nature of sin.

III. Peter's Repentance

Peter denied his Lord thrice, and then the Lord looked upon him. And that look of Jesus broke the heart of Peter, and all at once there opened up before him the terrible sin that he had committed, the terrible failure that had come, and the depth into which he had fallen, and "Peter went out and wept bitterly."

Oh, who can tell what that repentance must have been? During the following hours of that night, and the next day, when he saw Christ crucified and buried, and the next day, the Sabbath—oh, in what hopeless despair and shame he must have spent that day!

"My Lord is gone, my hope is gone, and I denied my Lord. After that life of love, after that blessed fellowship of three years, I denied my Lord. God have mercy upon me!"

I do not think we can realize into what a depth of humiliation Peter sank then. But that was the turning point and the change, and on the first day of the week Christ was seen of Peter, and in the evening he met him with the others. Later on, at the Lake of Galilee, he asked him, "Do you love me?" until Peter was made sad by the thought that the Lord reminded him of having denied him thrice and said in sorrow but in uprightness: "Lord, you know all things; you know that I love you" (John 21:17).

IV. Peter's Deliverance from Self

Now Peter was prepared for deliverance from self, and that is my last thought. You know Christ took him with others to the footstool of the throne and bade them wait there. And then on the day of Pentecost the Holy Spirit came, and Peter was a changed man. I do not want you to think only of the change in Peter, in that boldness, and that power, and that insight into the Scriptures, and that blessing with which he preached that day. Thank God for that. But there was something for Peter deeper and better. Peter's whole nature was changed. The work that Christ began in Peter when he looked upon him was perfected when he was filled with the Holy Spirit.

If you want to see that, read the First Epistle of Peter. You know wherein Peter's failings lay. When he said to Christ, in effect, "You never can suffer; it cannot be," it showed he had not a conception of what it was to pass through death into life. Christ said, "Deny yourself," and in spite of that, he denied his Lord. When Christ warned him, "You shall deny me," and he insisted that he never would, Peter showed how little he understood what there was in himself. But when I read his epistle and hear him say, "If you are reproached for the name of Christ, happy are you, for the Spirit of God and of glory rests upon you" (1 Peter 4:14), then I say that it is not the old Peter, but that is the very Spirit of Christ breathing and speaking within him.

I read again how he says, "Hereunto you are called to suffer, even as Christ suffered" (1 Peter 2:21). I understand what a change had come over Peter. Instead of denying Christ, he found joy and pleasure in having self denied and crucified and given up to the death. And therefore it is in the Acts we read that, when he was called before the Council, he could boldly say, "We must obey God rather than men" (Acts 5:29), and that he could return with the other disciples and rejoice that they were counted worthy to suffer for Christ's name.

You remember his self-exaltation. But now he has found out that "the ornament of a meek and quiet spirit is in the sight of God of great price." Again he tells us to be "subject one to another, and be clothed with humility" (1 Peter 5:5).

Dear friend, I beseech you, look at Peter utterly changed—the self-pleasing, the self-trusting, the self-seeking Peter, full of sin, continually getting into trouble, foolish and impetuous, but now filled with the Spirit and the life of Jesus. Christ had done it for him by the Holy Spirit.

And now, what is my object in having thus very briefly pointed to the story of Peter? That story must be the history of every believer who is really to be made a blessing by God. That story is a prophecy of what everyone can receive from God in Heaven.

Now let us just glance hurriedly at what these lessons teach us.

The first lesson is this: you may be a very earnest, godly, devoted believer, yet one in whom the power of the flesh is yet very strong.

That is a very solemn truth. Peter, before he denied Christ, had cast out devils and had healed the sick, and yet the flesh had power, and the flesh had room in him. Oh, beloved, we have to realize that it is just because there is so much of that self-life in us that the power of God cannot work in us as mightily as God is willing that it should work. Do you realize that the great God is longing to double his blessing, to give tenfold blessing through us? But there is something hindering him, and that something is a proof of nothing but the self-life. We talk about the pride of Peter, and the impetuosity of Peter, and the self-confidence of Peter. It all rooted in that one word, "self." Christ had said, "Deny self," and Peter had never understood and never obeyed. And every failing came out of that.

What a solemn thought, and what an urgent plea for us to cry, "O God, do reveal this to us, that none of us may be living the self-life!" It has happened to many a one who had been a Christian for years, who had perhaps occupied a prominent position, that God found him out and taught him to find himself out, and he became utterly ashamed, falling down broken before God. Oh, the bitter shame and sorrow and pain and agony that came to him, until at last he found that there was deliverance!

Peter went out and wept bitterly, and there may be many a godly one in whom the power of the flesh still rules.

And then my second lesson is: It is the work of our blessed Lord Jesus to reveal the power of self.

How was it that Peter, the carnal Peter, self-willed Peter, Peter with the strong self-love, ever became a man of Pentecost and the writer of his epistles? It was because Christ had him in charge, and Christ watched over him, and Christ taught and blessed him. The warnings that Christ had given him were part of the training; and last of all there came that look of love. In his suffering Christ did not forget him, but turned round and looked upon him, and "Peter went out and wept bitterly." And the Christ who led Peter to Pentecost is waiting today to take charge of every heart that is willing to surrender itself to him.

Are there not some saying: "Ah, that is the mischief with me; it is always the self-life and self-comfort and self-consciousness and self-pleasing and self-will; how am I to get rid of it?"

My answer is: It is Christ Jesus who can rid you of it; none else but Christ Jesus can give deliverance from the power of self. And what does he ask you to do? He asks that you should humble yourself before him.

Impossible with Man, Possible with God

*"And he said, The things which are impossible with men
are possible with God."*
—Luke 18:27

Christ had said to the rich young ruler, "Sell all that you have . . . and come, follow me." The young man went away sorrowful. Christ then turned to the disciples and said, "How hardly shall they that have riches enter into the kingdom of God!" The disciples, we read, were greatly astonished and answered: "If it is so difficult to enter the kingdom, who, then, can be saved?" And Christ gave this blessed answer: "The things which are impossible with men are possible with God."

The text contains two thoughts: that in religion, in the question of salvation and of following Christ by a holy life, it is impossible for man to do it; and then alongside that is the thought, What is impossible with man is possible with God.

The two thoughts mark the two great lessons that man has to learn in the religious life. It often takes a long time to learn the first lesson, that in religion man can do nothing—that salvation is impossible to man. And often a man learns that and yet he does not learn the second lesson: what has been impossible to him is possible with God. Blessed is the man who learns both lessons! The learning of them marks stages in the Christian's life.

I

The one stage is when a man is trying to do his utmost and fails, when a man tries to do better and fails again, when a man tries much more and always fails. And yet very often he does not even then learn the lesson:

126 ❀

With man it is impossible to serve God and Christ. Peter spent three years in Christ's school, and he never learned that it is impossible until he had denied his Lord and went out and wept bitterly. Then he learned it.

Just look for a moment at a man who is learning this lesson. At first he fights against it; then he submits to it, but reluctantly and in despair; at last he accepts it willingly and rejoices in it. At the beginning of the Christian life, the young convert has no conception of this truth. He has been converted; he has the joy of the Lord in his heart; he begins to run the race and fight the battle; he is sure he can conquer, for he is earnest and honest, and God will help him. Yet, somehow, very soon he fails where he did not expect it, and sin gets the better of him. He is disappointed. But he thinks: "I was not watchful enough; I did not make my resolutions strong enough." And again he vows, and again he prays, and yet he fails. He thinks: "Am I not a regenerate man? Have I not the life of God within me?" And he thinks again, "Yes, and I have Christ to help me; I can live the holy life."

At a later period, he comes to another state of mind. He begins to see such a life is impossible, but he does not accept it. There are multitudes of Christians who come to this point, "I cannot," and then think God never expected them to do what they cannot do. If you tell them that God does expect it, it appears to them a mystery. A good many Christians are living a low life, a life of failure and of sin instead of rest and victory, because they began to see, "I cannot; it is impossible." And yet they do not understand it fully, and so under the impression, "I cannot," they give way to despair. They will do their best, but they never expect to get on very far.

But God leads his children on to a third stage, when a man comes to take that "it is impossible" in its full truth and yet at the same time says: "I must do it, and I will do it; it is impossible for man, and yet I must do it"—when the renewed will begins to exercise its whole power and in intense longing and prayer begins to cry to God: "Lord, what is the meaning of this? How am I to be freed from the power of sin?"

It is the state of the regenerate man in Romans 7. There you will find the Christian man trying his very utmost to live a holy life. God's law has been revealed to him as reaching down into the very depth of the desires of the heart, and the man can dare to say: "I delight in the law of God after the inward man. To will what is good is present with me. My heart loves the law of God, and my will has chosen that law."

Can a man like that fail with his heart full of delight in God's law and with his will determined to do what is right? Yes. That is what Romans 7 teaches us. There is something more needed. Not only must I delight in the law of God after the inward man, and will what God wills, but I need a divine omnipotence to work it in me. And that is what the apostle Paul teaches in Philippians 2:13: "It is God which works in you, both to will and to do."

Note the contrast. In Romans 7, the regenerate man says: "To will is present with me, but to do—I find I cannot do. I will, but I cannot perform." But in Philippians 2, you have a man who has been led on farther, a man who understands that when God has worked the renewed will, God will give the power to accomplish what that will desires. Let us receive this as the first great lesson in the spiritual life: "It is impossible for me, my God; let there be an end of the flesh and all its powers, an end of self, and let it be my glory to be helpless."

Praise God for the divine teaching that makes us helpless!

When you thought of absolute surrender to God, were you not brought to an end of yourself and to feel that you could see how you actually could live as a man absolutely surrendered to God every moment of the day—at your table, in your house, in your business, in the midst of trials and temptations? I pray you learn the lesson now. If you felt you could not do it, you are on the right road—if you let yourselves be led. Accept that position, and maintain it before God: "My heart's desire and delight, O God, is absolute surrender, but I cannot perform it. It is impossible for me to live that life. It is beyond me." Fall down and learn that when you are utterly helpless, God will come to work in you not only to will, but also to do.

II

Now comes the second lesson: "The things which are impossible with men are possible with God."

I said a little while ago that there is many a man who has learned the lesson, "It is impossible with men," and then he gives up in helpless despair and lives a wretched Christian life without joy or strength or victory. And why? Because he does not humble himself to learn that other lesson—with God all things are possible.

Your religious life is every day to be a proof that God works impossibilities; your religious life is to be a series of impossibilities made possible and actual by God's almighty power. That is what the Christian needs. He has an almighty God that he worships, and he must learn to understand that he does not need a little of God's power, but he needs—with reverence be it said—the whole of God's omnipotence to keep him right and to live like a Christian.

The whole of Christianity is a work of God's omnipotence. Look at the birth of Christ Jesus. That was a miracle of divine power, and it was said to Mary, "With God nothing shall be impossible." It was the omnipotence of God. Look at Christ's resurrection. We are taught that it was according to the exceeding greatness of his mighty power that God raised Christ from the dead.

Every tree must grow on the root from which it springs. An oak tree three hundred years old grows all the time on the one root from which it had its beginning. Christianity had its beginning in the omnipotence of God, and in every soul it must have its continuance in that omnipotence. All the possibilities of the higher Christian life have their origin in a new apprehension of Christ's power to work all God's will in us.

I want to call upon you now to come and worship an almighty God. Have you learned to do it? Have you learned to deal so closely with an almighty God that you know omnipotence is working in you? In outward appearance, there is often so little sign of it. The apostle Paul said: "I was with you in weakness and in fear and in much trembling, and . . . my preaching was . . . in demonstration of the Spirit and of power." From the human side there was feebleness; from the divine side there was divine omnipotence. And that is true of every godly life, and if we would only learn that lesson better and give a wholehearted, undivided surrender to it, we should learn what blessedness there is in dwelling every hour and every moment with an almighty God.

Have you ever studied in the Bible the attribute of God's omnipotence? you know that it was God's omnipotence that created the world and created light out of darkness and created man. But have you studied God's omnipotence in the works of redemption?

Look at Abraham. When God called him to be the father of that people out of which Christ was to be born, God said to him: "I am God Almighty; walk before me and be perfect." And God trained Abraham to trust him as the omnipotent One. And whether it was his going out to a land that he knew not or his faith as a pilgrim amid the thousands of Canaanites, his faith said: "This is my land." Or whether it was his faith in waiting twenty-five years for a son in his old age, against all hope, or whether it was the raising up of Isaac from the dead on Mount Moriah when he was going to sacrifice him, Abraham believed God. He was strong in faith, giving glory to God, because he accounted him who had promised able to perform.

The cause of the weakness of your Christian life is that you want to work it out partly and to let God "help" you. And that cannot be. You must come to be utterly helpless, to let God work, and God will work gloriously. It is this that we need if we are indeed to be workers for God. I could go through Scripture and prove to you how Moses, when he led Israel out of Egypt—how Joshua, when he brought them into the land of Canaan—how all God's servants in the Old Testament counted upon the omnipotence of God doing impossibilities. And this God lives today, and this God is the God of every child of his. And yet we are, some of us, wanting God to give us a little help while we do our best, instead of coming to understand what God wants and to say: "I can do nothing. God must, and will, do all." Have you said, "In worship, in work, in sanctification, in obedience to God, I can do nothing of myself, and so my place is to worship the omnipotent God, and to believe that he will work in me every moment"? Oh, may God teach us this! Oh, that God would by his grace show you what a God you have, and to what a God you have entrusted yourself—an omnipotent God, willing with his whole omnipotence to place himself at the disposal of every child of his! Shall we not take the lesson of the Lord Jesus and say: "Amen; the things which are impossible with men are possible with God"?

Remember what we have said about Peter, his self-confidence, self-power, self-will, and how he came to deny his Lord. You feel, "Ah, there is the self-life; there is the flesh-life that rules in me!" And now, have you believed that there is deliverance from that? Have you believed that Almighty God is able so to reveal Christ in your heart, so to let the Holy Spirit rule in you that the self-life shall not have power or dominion over you? Have you coupled the two together and with tears of penitence and with deep humiliation and feebleness cried out: "O God, it is impossible to me; man cannot do it, but, glory to your name, it is possible with God"? Have you claimed deliverance? Do it now. Put yourself afresh in absolute surrender into the hands of a God of infinite love. And as infinite as his love is his power to do it.

But again, we came to the question of absolute surrender, and felt that that is the want in the Church of Christ, and that is why the Holy Spirit cannot fill us, and why we cannot live as people entirely separated unto the Holy Spirit. That is why the flesh and the self-life cannot be conquered. We have never understood what it is to be absolutely surrendered to God as Jesus was. I know that many a one earnestly and honestly says, "Amen; I accept the message of absolute surrender to God," and yet thinks: "Will that ever be mine? Can I count upon God to make me one of whom it shall be said in Heaven and on earth and in Hell, he lives in absolute surrender to God?" Brother, sister, "the things which are impossible with men are possible with God." Do believe that when he takes charge of you in Christ, it is possible for God to make you a man or woman of absolute surrender. And God is able to maintain that. He is able to let you rise from bed every morning of the week with that blessed thought directly or indirectly: "I am in God's charge. My God is working out my life for me."

Some are weary of thinking about sanctification. You pray, you have longed and cried for it, and yet it appeared so far off! The holiness and humility of Jesus—you are so conscious of how distant it is. Beloved friends, the one doctrine of sanctification that is scriptural and real and effectual is this: "The things which are impossible with men are possible with God." God can sanctify men and women, and by his almighty and sanctifying power every moment, God can keep them. Oh, that we might get a step nearer to our God now! Oh, that the light of God might shine, and that we might know our God better!

I could go on to speak about the life of Christ in us—living like Christ, taking Christ as our Savior from sin and as our life and strength. It is God in Heaven who can reveal that in you. What does that prayer of the apostle Paul say: "That he would grant you according to the riches of his glory." It is sure to be something very wonderful if it is according to the riches of his glory, "to be strengthened with might by his Spirit in the inner man." Do you not see that it is an omnipotent God working by his omnipotence in the heart of his believing children, so that Christ can become an indwelling Savior? You have tried to grasp it and to seize it, and you have tried to believe it, and it would not come. It was because you had not been brought to believe that "the things which are impossible with men are possible with God."

And so, I trust that the word spoken about love may have brought many to see that we must have an inflowing of love in quite a new way: our heart must be filled with life from above, from the Fountain of everlasting love, if it is going to overflow all the day. Then it will be just as natural for us to love our fellow men and women as it is natural for the lamb to be gentle and the wolf to be cruel. Until I am brought to such a state that the more someone hates and speaks evil of me, the more unlikable and unlovable someone is, I shall love them all the more, until I am brought to such a state that the more the obstacles and hatred and ingratitude, the more can the power of love triumph in me. Until I am brought to see that, I am not saying: "It is impossible with men." But if you have been led to say: "This message has spoken to me about a love utterly beyond my power; it is absolutely impossible"—then we can come to God and say, "It is possible with you."

Some are crying to God for a great revival. I can say that that is the prayer of my heart unceasingly. Oh, if God would only revive his believing people! I cannot think in the first place of the unconverted formalists of the Church, or of the infidels and skeptics, or of all the wretched and perishing around me. My heart prays in the first place, "My God, revive your Church and people." It is not for nothing that there are in thousands of hearts yearnings after holiness and consecration: it is a forerunner of God's power. God works to will, and then he works to do. These yearnings are a witness and a proof that God has worked to will. Oh, let us in faith believe that the omnipotent God will work to do among his people more than we can ask. "Unto him," Paul said, "who is able to do exceeding abundantly above all that we ask or think. . . . unto him be glory." Let our hearts say that. Glory to God, the omnipotent One, who can do above what we dare to ask or think!

"The things which are impossible with men are possible with God." All around you there is a world of sin and sorrow, and the Devil is there. But remember, Christ is on the throne; Christ is stronger; Christ has conquered; and Christ will conquer. But wait on God. My text casts us down: "The things which are impossible with men"—but it ultimately lifts us up high—"are possible with God." Get linked to God. Adore and trust him as the omnipotent One, not only for your own life, but for all the souls that are entrusted to you. Never pray without adoring his omnipotence, saying: "Mighty God, I claim your almightiness." And the answer to the prayer will come, and like Abraham you will become strong in faith, giving glory to God, because you account him who has promised able to perform.

O Wretched Man That I Am!

"O wretched man that I am! Who shall deliver me
from the body of this death? I thank God
through Jesus Christ our Lord."
—*Romans 7:24–25*

You know the wonderful place that this text has in the wonderful epistle to the Romans. It stands here at the end of the seventh chapter as the gateway into the eighth. In the first sixteen verses of the eighth chapter, the name of the Holy Spirit is found sixteen times; you have there the description and promise of the life that a child of God can live in the power of the Holy Spirit. This begins in the second verse: "The law of the Spirit of life in Christ Jesus has made me free from the law of sin and death" (Romans 8:12). From that Paul goes on to speak of the great privileges of the child of God, who is to be led by the Spirit of God. The gateway into all this is in the twenty-fourth verse of the seventh chapter: "O wretched man that I am!"

There you have the words of a man who has come to the end of himself. He has in the previous verses described how he had struggled and wrestled in his own power to obey the holy law of God and had failed. But in answer to his own question, he now finds the true answer and cries out: "I thank God through Jesus Christ our Lord." From that he goes on to speak of what that deliverance is that he has found.

I want from these words to describe the path by which a man can be led out of the spirit of bondage into the spirit of liberty. You know how distinctly it is said, "You have not received the spirit of bondage again to fear." We are continually warned that this is the great danger of the Christian life—to go again into bondage. And I want to describe the path by which a man can get out of bondage into the glorious liberty of the children of God. Rather, I want to describe the man himself.

First, these words are the language of a regenerate man; second, of an impotent man; third, of a wretched man; and fourth, of a man on the borders of complete liberty.

I.   *The Regenerate Man*

There is much evidence of regeneration from the fourteenth verse of the chapter on to the twenty-third. "It is no more I that do it, but sin that dwells in me" (Romans 7:17): that is the language of a regenerate man, a man who knows that his heart and nature have been renewed, and that sin is now a power in him that is not himself. "I delight in the law of the Lord after the inward man" (Romans 7:22): that again is the language of a regenerate man. He dares to say when he does evil, "It is no more I that do it, but sin that dwells in me." It is of great importance to understand this.

In the first two great sections of the epistle, Paul deals with justification and sanctification. In dealing with justification, he lays the foundation of the doctrine in the teaching about sin, not in the singular, sin, but in the plural, sins—the actual transgressions. In the second part of the fifth chapter, he begins to deal with sin, not as actual transgression, but as a power. Just imagine what a loss it would have been to us if we had not this second half of the seventh chapter of the Epistle to the Romans—if Paul had omitted in his teaching this vital question of the sinfulness of the believer. We should have missed the question we all want answered as to sin in the believer. What is the answer? The regenerate man is one in whom the will has been renewed and who can say, "I delight in the law of God after the inward man."

II.   *The Impotent Man*

Here is the great mistake made by many Christian people: they think that when there is a renewed will, it is enough. But that is not the case. This regenerate man tells us, "I will to do what is good, but the power to perform I find not." How often people tell us that if you set yourself determinedly, you can perform what you will! But this man was as determined as any man can be, and yet he made the confession, "To will is present with me; but how to perform that which is good, I find not" (Romans 7:18).

But, you ask, "How is it God makes a regenerate man utter such a confession, with a right will, with a heart that longs to do good and longs to do its very utmost to love God?"

Let us look at this question. What has God given us our will for? Had the angels who fell, in their own will, the strength to stand? Surely not. The will of the creature is nothing but an empty vessel in which the power of God is to be made manifest. The creature must seek in God all that it is to be. You have it in the second chapter of the Epistle to the Philippians, and you have it here also, that God's work is to work in us both to will and to do of his good pleasure. Here is a man who appears to say, "God has not worked to do in me." But we are taught that God works both to will and to do. How is the apparent contradiction to be reconciled?

You will find that in this passage (Romans 7:6–25), the name of the Holy Spirit does not occur once, nor does the name of Christ occur. The man is wrestling and struggling to fulfill God's law. Instead of the Holy Spirit and Christ, the law is mentioned nearly twenty times. In this chapter, it shows a believer doing his very best to obey the law of God with his regenerate will. Not only this, but you will find the little words "I," "me," "my" occur more than forty times. It is the regenerate "I" in its impotence seeking to obey the law without being filled with the Spirit. This is the experience of almost every saint. After conversion a man begins to do his best, and he fails. But if we are brought into the full light, we need fail no longer. Nor need we fail at all if we have received the Spirit in his fullness at conversion.

God allows that failure that the regenerate man should be taught his own utter impotence. It is in the course of this struggle that there comes to us this sense of our utter sinfulness. It is God's way of dealing with us. He allows that man to strive to fulfill the law that, as he strives and wrestles, he may be brought to this: "I am a regenerate child of God, but I am utterly helpless to obey his law." See what strong words are used all through the chapter to describe this condition: "I am carnal, sold under sin" (Romans 7:14); "I see another law in my members bringing me into captivity" (Romans 7:23); and last of all, "O wretched man that I am! Who shall deliver me from the body of this death?" (Romans 7:24). This believer who bows here in deep contrition is utterly unable to obey the law of God.

III. The Wretched Man

Not only is the man who makes this confession a regenerate and an impotent man, but he is also a wretched man. He is utterly unhappy and miserable. And what is it that makes him so utterly miserable? It is because God has given him a nature that loves himself. He is deeply wretched because he feels he is not obeying his God. He says with brokenness of heart: "It is not I that do it, but I am under the awful power of sin, which is holding me down. It is I, and yet not I: alas, alas, it is myself; so closely am I bound up with it, and so closely is it intertwined with my very nature." Blessed be God when a man learns to say, "O wretched man that I am!" from the depth of his heart. He is on the way to the eighth chapter of Romans.

There are many who make this confession a pillow for sin. They say that if Paul had to confess his weakness and helplessness in this way, what are they that they should try to do better? So the call to holiness is quietly set aside. Would to God that every one of us had learned to say these words in the very spirit in which they are written here! When we hear sin spoken of as the abominable thing that God hates, do not many of us wince before the word? Would that all Christians who go on sinning and sinning would take this verse to heart. If ever you utter a sharp word, say: "O wretched man that I am!" And every time you lose your temper, kneel down and understand that it never was meant by God that this was to be the state in which his child should remain. Would God that we would take this word into our daily life, and say it every time we are touched about our own honor, and every time we say sharp things, and every time we sin against the Lord God and against the Lord Jesus Christ in his humility and in his obedience and in his self-sacrifice! Would to God you could forget everything else, and cry out: "O wretched man that I am! Who shall deliver me from the body of this death?"

Why should you say this whenever you commit sin? Because it is when a man is brought to this confession that deliverance is at hand.

And remember it was not only the sense of being impotent and taken captive that made him wretched, but it was above all the sense of sinning against his God. The law was doing its work, making sin exceedingly sinful in his sight. The thought of continually grieving God became utterly unbearable—it was this that brought forth the piercing cry, "O wretched man!" As long as we talk and reason about our impotence and our failure, and only try to find out what Romans 7 means, it will profit us but little.

But when once every sin gives new intensity to the sense of wretchedness, and we feel our whole state as one of not only helplessness but actual exceeding sinfulness, we shall be pressed not only to ask, "Who shall deliver us?" but to cry, "I thank God through Jesus Christ my Lord."

IV.   *The Almost-Delivered Man*

The man has tried to obey the beautiful law of God. He has loved it, he has wept over his sin, he has tried to conquer, he has tried to overcome fault after fault, but every time he has ended in failure.

What did he mean by "the body of this death"? Did he mean, my body when I die? Surely not. In the eighth chapter you have the answer to this question in the words, "If you through the Spirit do mortify the deeds of the body, you shall live." That is the body of death from which he is seeking deliverance.

And now he is on the brink of deliverance! In the twenty-third verse of the seventh chapter, we have the words: "I see another law in my members, warring against the law of my mind, and bringing me into captivity to the law of sin which is in my members." It is a captive that cries: "O wretched man that I am! Who shall deliver me from the body of this death?" He is a man who feels himself bound. But look to the contrast in the second verse of the eighth chapter: "The law of the Spirit of life in Christ Jesus has made me free from the law of sin and death." That is the deliverance through Jesus Christ our Lord—the liberty to the captive which the Spirit brings. Can you keep captive any longer a man made free by the "law of the Spirit of life in Christ Jesus"?

But you say: the regenerate man, had not he the Spirit of Jesus when he spoke in the sixth chapter? Yes, but he did not know what the Holy Spirit could do for him.

God does not work by his Spirit as he works by a blind force in nature. He leads his people on as reasonable, intelligent beings, and therefore when he wants to give us that Holy Spirit whom he has promised, he brings us first to the end of self, to the conviction that though we have been striving to obey the law, we have failed. When we have come to the end of that, then he shows us that in the Holy Spirit we have the power of obedience, the power of victory, and the power of real holiness.

God works to will, and he is ready to work to do, but alas, many Christians misunderstand this. They think because they have the will, it is enough, and that now they are able to do. This is not so. The new will is a permanent gift, an attribute of the new nature. The power to do is not a permanent gift, but must be each moment received from the Holy Spirit. It is the man who is conscious of his own impotence as a believer who will learn that by the Holy Spirit he can live a holy life. This man is on the brink of that great deliverance; the way has been prepared for the glorious eighth chapter. I now ask this solemn question: Where are you living? Is it with you, "O wretched man that I am! Who shall deliver me?" With now and then a little experience of the power of the Holy Spirit? Or is it, "I thank God through Jesus Christ! The law of the Spirit has set me free from the law of sin and of death"?

What the Holy Spirit does is to give the victory. "If you through the Spirit do mortify the deeds of the flesh, you shall live" (Romans 8:13). It is the Holy Spirit who does this—the third Person of the Godhead. He it is who, when the heart is opened wide to receive him, comes in and reigns there and mortifies the deeds of the body, day by day, hour by hour, and moment by moment.

I want to bring this to a point. Remember, dear friend, what we need is to come to decision and action. There are in Scripture two very different sorts of Christians. The Bible speaks in Romans, Corinthians, and Galatians about yielding to the flesh, and that is the life of tens of thousands of believers. All their lack of joy in the Holy Spirit, and their lack of the liberty he gives, is just owing to the flesh. The Spirit is within them, but the flesh rules the life. To be led by the Spirit of God is what they need. Would God that I could make every child of his realize what it means that the everlasting God has given his dear Son, Christ Jesus, to watch over you every day, and that what you have to do is to trust, and that the work of the Holy Spirit is to enable you every moment to remember Jesus and to trust him! The Spirit has come to keep the link with him unbroken every moment. Praise God for the Holy Spirit! We are so accustomed to think of the Holy Spirit as a luxury for special times or for special ministers and men and women. But the Holy Spirit is necessary for every believer, every moment of the day. Praise God you have him, and that he gives you the full experience of the deliverance in Christ, as he makes you free from the power of sin.

Who longs to have the power and the liberty of the Holy Spirit? Oh, brother, bow before God in one final cry of despair: "O God, must I go on sinning this way forever? Who shall deliver me, O wretched man that I am, from the body of this death?"

Are you ready to sink before God in that cry and seek the power of Jesus to dwell and work in you? Are you ready to say, "I thank God through Jesus Christ"?

What good does it do that we go to church or attend conventions, that we study our Bibles and pray, unless our lives are filled with the Holy Spirit? That is what God wants, and nothing else will enable us to live a life of power and peace. You know that when a minister or parent is using the Catechism, when a question is asked an answer is expected. Alas, how many Christians are content with the question put here, "O wretched man that I am! Who shall deliver me from the body of this death?" but never give the answer. Instead of answering, they are silent; instead of saying, "I thank God through Jesus Christ our Lord," they are forever repeating the question without the answer. If you want the path to the full deliverance of Christ and the liberty of the Spirit, the glorious liberty of the children of God, take it through the seventh chapter of Romans. And then say, "I thank God through Jesus Christ our Lord." Be not content to remain ever groaning, but say: "I, a wretched man, thank God, through Jesus Christ. Even though I do not see it all, I am going to praise God."

There is deliverance, there is the liberty of the Holy Spirit. The kingdom of God is "joy in the Holy Spirit" (Romans 14:17).

Having Begun in the Spirit

The words from which I wish to address you, you will find in the epistle to the Galatians, the third chapter, the third verse; let us read the second verse also: "This only would I learn of you, Received you the Spirit by the works of the law, or by the hearing of faith? Are you so foolish?" And then comes my text—"Having begun in the Spirit, are you now made perfect by the flesh?"

When we speak of the quickening or the deepening or the strengthening of the spiritual life, we are thinking of something that is feeble and wrong and sinful. And it is a great thing to take our place before God with the confession, "O God, our spiritual life is not what it should be!"

May God work that in your heart, reader.

As we look round about on the church, we see so many indications of feebleness and of failure, and of sin and of shortcoming, that we are compelled to ask: Why is it? Is there any necessity for the church of Christ to be living in such a low state? Or is it actually possible that God's people should be living always in the joy and strength of their God?

Every believing heart must answer: It is possible.

Then comes the great question: Why is it—how is it to be accounted for—that God's church as a whole is so feeble, and that the great majority of Christians are not living up to their privileges? There must be a reason for it. Has God not given Christ his Almighty Son to be the Keeper of every believer, to make Christ an ever-present reality, and to impart and communicate to us all that we have in Christ? God has given his Son, and God has given his Spirit. How is it that believers do not live up to their privileges?

We find in more than one of the epistles a very solemn answer to that question. There are epistles, such as the first to the Thessalonians, where

Paul writes to the Christians, in effect: "I want you to grow, to abound, to increase more and more." They were young, and there were things lacking in their faith, but their state was so far satisfactory and gave him great joy, and he writes time after time: "I pray God that you may abound more and more; I write to you to increase more and more" (1 Thessalonians 4:1, 10). But there are other epistles where he takes a very different tone, especially the epistles to the Corinthians and to the Galatians, and he tells them in many different ways what the one reason was that they were not living as Christians ought to live. Many were under the power of the flesh. My text is one example. He reminds them that by the preaching of faith, they had received the Holy Spirit. He had preached Christ to them; they had accepted that Christ, and had received the Holy Spirit in power. But what happened? Having begun in the Spirit, they tried to perfect the work that the Spirit had begun in the flesh by their own effort. We find the same teaching in the epistle to the Corinthians.

Now, we have here a solemn discovery of what the great want is in the church of Christ. God has called the church of Christ to live in the power of the Holy Spirit, and the church is living for the most part in the power of human flesh and of will and energy and effort apart from the Spirit of God. I doubt not that that is the case with many individual believers. And, oh, if God will use me to give you a message from him, my one message will be this: "If the church will return to acknowledge that the Holy Spirit is her strength and her help, and if the church will return to give up everything and wait upon God to be filled with the Spirit, her days of beauty and gladness will return, and we shall see the glory of God revealed among us." This is my message to every individual believer: "Nothing will help you unless you come to understand that you must live every day under the power of the Holy Spirit."

God wants you to be a living vessel in whom the power of the Spirit is to be manifested every hour and every moment of your life, and God will enable you to be that.

Now let us try to learn that this word to the Galatians teaches us—some very simple thoughts. It shows us how (1) the beginning of the Christian life is receiving the Holy Spirit. It shows us (2) what great danger there is of forgetting that we are to live by the Spirit, and not live after the flesh. It shows us (3) what are the fruits and the proofs of our seeking perfection in the flesh. And then it suggests to us (4) the way of deliverance from this state.

I. Receiving the Holy Spirit

First of all, Paul says: "Having begun in the Spirit." Remember, the apostle not only preached justification by faith, but he preached something more. He preached this—the epistle is full of it—that justified men cannot live but by the Holy Spirit, and that therefore God gives to every justified man the Holy Spirit to seal him. The apostle says to them in effect more than once: "How did you receive the Holy Spirit? Was it by the preaching of the law, or by the preaching of faith?"

He could point back to that time when there had been a mighty revival under his teaching. The power of God had been manifested, and the Galatians were compelled to confess: "Yes, we have got the Holy Spirit: accepting Christ by faith, by faith we received the Holy Spirit."

Now, it is to be feared that there are many Christians who hardly know that when they believed, they received the Holy Spirit. A great many Christians can say, "I received pardon, and I received peace." But if you were to ask them, "Have you received the Holy Spirit," they would hesitate, and many, if they were to say, "Yes," would say it with hesitation. And they would tell you that they hardly knew what it was, since that time, to walk in the power of the Holy Spirit. Let us try and take hold of this great truth: The beginning of the true Christian life is to receive the Holy Spirit. And the work of every Christian minister is that which was the work of Paul—to remind his people that they received the Holy Spirit and must live according to his guidance and in his power.

If those Galatians who received the Holy Spirit in power were tempted to go astray by that terrible danger of perfecting in the flesh what had been begun in the Spirit, how much more danger do those Christians run who hardly ever know that they have received the Holy Spirit or who, if they know it as a matter of belief, hardly ever think of it and hardly ever praise God for it!

II. Neglecting the Holy Spirit

But now look, in the second place, at the great danger.

You all know what shunting is on a railroad. A locomotive with its train may be run in a certain direction, and the points at some place may not be properly opened or closed, and unobservingly it is shunted off to the right or to the left. And if that takes place, for instance, on a dark night, the train goes in the wrong direction, and the people might never know it until they have gone some distance.

And just so God gives Christians the Holy Spirit with this intention: that every day, all their life should be lived in the power of the Spirit. A man cannot live one hour a godly life unless by the power of the Holy Spirit. He may live a proper, consistent life, as people call it, an irreproachable life, a life of virtue and diligent service. But to live a life acceptable to God, in the enjoyment of God's salvation and God's love, to live and walk in the power of the new life, he cannot do it unless he be guided by the Holy Spirit every day and every hour.

But now listen to the danger. The Galatians received the Holy Spirit, but what was begun by the Spirit they tried to perfect in the flesh. How? They fell back again under Judaizing teachers who told them they must be circumcised. They began to seek their religion in external observances. And so Paul uses that expression about those teachers who had them circumcised, that "they sought to glory in their flesh" (Galatians 6:13).

You sometimes hear the expression used, "religious flesh." What is meant by that? It is simply an expression made to give utterance to this thought: "My human nature and my human will and my human effort can be very active in religion, and after being converted, and after receiving the Holy Spirit, I may begin in my own strength to try to serve God."

I may be very diligent and doing a great deal, and yet all the time it is more the work of human flesh than of God's Spirit. What a solemn thought, that man can, without noticing it, be shunted off from the line of the Holy Spirit on to the line of the flesh—that he can be most diligent and make great sacrifices, and yet it is all in the power of the human will! Ah, the great question for us to ask of God in self-examination is that we may be shown whether our religious life is lived more in the power of the flesh than in the power of the Holy Spirit. A man may be a preacher, he may work most diligently in his ministry, a man may be a Christian worker, and others may tell of him that he makes great sacrifices, and yet you can feel there is a want about it. You feel that he is not a spiritual man; there is no spirituality about his life. How many Christians there are about whom no one would ever think of saying, "What a spiritual man he is!" Ah, there is the weakness of the Church of Christ. It is all in that one word, "flesh."

Now, the flesh may manifest itself in many ways. It may be manifested in fleshly wisdom. My mind may be most active about religion. I may preach or write or think or meditate, and delight in being occupied with things in God's Book and in God's Kingdom, and yet the power of the

Holy Spirit may be markedly absent. I fear that if you take the preaching throughout the Church of Christ and ask why there is, alas, so little converting power in the preaching of the Word, why there is so much work and often so little result for eternity, why the Word has so little power to build up believers in holiness and in consecration, the answer will come: It is the absence of the power of the Holy Spirit. And why is this? There can be no other reason but that the flesh and human energy have taken the place that the Holy Spirit ought to have. That was true of the Galatians; it was true of the Corinthians. You know Paul said to them: "I cannot speak to you as to spiritual men; you ought to be spiritual men, but you are carnal." And you know how often in the course of his epistles he had to reprove and condemn them for strife and for divisions.

III.   Lacking the Fruit of the Holy Spirit

A third thought: What are the proofs or indications that a church like the Galatians, or a Christian, is serving God in the power of the flesh—is perfecting in the flesh what was begun in the Spirit?

The answer is very easy. Religious self-effort always ends in sinful flesh. What was the state of those Galatians? Striving to be justified by the works of the law. And yet they were quarreling and in danger of devouring one another. Count up the expressions that the apostle uses to indicate their want of love, and you will find more than twelve—envy, jealousy, bitterness, strife, and all sorts of expressions. Read in the fourth and fifth chapters what he says about that. You see how they tried to serve God in their own strength, and they failed utterly. All this religious effort resulted in failure. The power of sin and the sinful flesh got the better of them, and their whole condition was one of the saddest that could be thought of.

This comes to us with unspeakable solemnity. There is a complaint everywhere in the Christian Church of the want of a high standard of integrity and godliness, even among the professing members of Christian churches. I remember a sermon which I heard preached on commercial morality. And, oh, if we speak not only of the commercial morality or immorality, but if we go into the homes of Christians, and if we think of the life to which God has called his children, and which he enables them to live by the Holy Spirit, and if we think of how much, nevertheless, there is of unlovingness and temper and sharpness and bitterness, and if we think how much there is very often of strife among the members of churches, and how much there is of envy and jealousy and sensitiveness and pride, then we are compelled to say: "Where are marks of the presence of the Spirit of the Lamb of God?" Wanting—sadly wanting!

Many people speak of these things as though they were the natural result of our feebleness and cannot well be helped. Many people speak of these things as sins, yet have given up the hope of conquering them. Many people speak of these things in the church around them and do not see the least prospect of ever having the things changed. There is no prospect until there comes a radical change—until the Church of God begins to see that every sin in the believer comes from the flesh, from a fleshly life amid our religious activities, from a striving in self-effort to serve God. Until we learn to make confession, and until we begin to see we must somehow or other get God's Spirit in power back to his Church, we must fail. Where did the Church begin in Pentecost? There they began in the Spirit. But, alas, how the Church of the next century went off into the flesh! They thought to perfect the Church in the flesh.

Do not let us think that because the blessed Reformation restored the great doctrine of justification by faith, the power of the Holy Spirit was then fully restored. If it is our faith that God is going to have mercy on his Church in these last ages, it will be because the doctrine and the truth about the Holy Spirit will not only be studied, but sought after with a whole heart—and not only because that truth will be sought after, but because ministers and congregations will be found bowing before God in deep abasement with one cry: "We have grieved God's Spirit; we have tried to be Christian churches with as little as possible of God's Spirit; we have not sought to be churches filled with the Holy Spirit."

All the feebleness in the Church is owing to the refusal of the Church to obey its God.

And why is that so? I know your answer. You say: "We are too feeble and too helpless, and we try to obey, and we vow to obey, but somehow we fail."

Ah, yes, you fail because you do not accept the strength of God. God alone can work out his will in you. You cannot work out God's will, but his Holy Spirit can. And until the Church—until believers—grasp this and cease trying by human effort to do God's will, and wait upon the Holy Spirit to come with all his omnipotent and enabling power, the Church will never be what God wants her to be, and what God is willing to make of her.

IV. Yielding to the Holy Spirit

I come now to my last thought, the question, What is the way to restoration?

Beloved friend, the answer is simple and easy. If that train has been shunted off, there is nothing for it but to come back to the point at which it was led away. The Galatians had no other way in returning but to come back to where they had gone wrong, to come back from all religious effort in their own strength and from seeking anything by their own work, and to yield themselves humbly to the Holy Spirit. There is no other way for us as individuals.

Is there any brother or sister whose heart is conscious, "Alas, my life knows but little of the power of the Holy Spirit"? I come to you with God's message that you can have no conception of what your life would be in the power of the Holy Spirit. It is too high and too blessed and too wonderful, but I bring you the message that just as truly as the everlasting Son of God came to this world and wrought his wonderful works, that just as truly as on Calvary he died and wrought out your redemption by his precious blood, so, just as truly, can the Holy Spirit come into your heart so that, with his divine power, he may sanctify you and enable you to do God's blessed will and fill your heart with joy and with strength. But, alas, we have forgotten, we have grieved, we have dishonored the Holy Spirit, and he has not been able to do his work. But I bring you the message: the Father in Heaven loves to fill his children with his Holy Spirit. God longs to give each one individually, separately, the power of the Holy Spirit for daily life. The command comes to us individually, unitedly. God wants us as his children to arise and place our sins before him and to call upon him for mercy. Oh, are you so foolish? Having begun in the Spirit, are you perfecting in the flesh that which was begun in the Spirit? Let us bow in shame and confess before God how our fleshly religion, our self-effort, and self-confidence have been the cause of every failure.

I have often been asked by young Christians: "Why is it that I fail so? I did so solemnly vow with my whole heart, and did desire to serve God; why have I failed?"

To such I always give the one answer: "My dear friend, you are trying to do in your own strength what Christ alone can do in you."

And when they tell me: "I am sure I knew Christ alone could do it; I was not trusting in myself," my answer always is: "You were trusting in yourself, or you could not have failed. If you had trusted Christ, he could not fail."

Oh, this perfecting in the flesh what was begun in the Spirit runs far deeper through us than we know. Let us ask God to reveal to us that it is only when we are brought to utter shame and emptiness that we shall be prepared to receive the blessing that comes from on high.

And so I come with these two questions. Are you living, beloved brother-minister—I ask it of every minister of the Gospel—are you living under the power of the Holy Spirit? Are you living as an anointed, Spirit-filled man in your ministry and your life before God? O brethren, our place is an awful one. We have to show people what God will do for us, not in our words and teaching, but in our life. God help us to do it!

I ask it of every member of Christ's Church and of every believer: Are you living a life under the power of the Holy Spirit day by day, or are you attempting to live without that? Remember you cannot. Are you consecrated, given up to the Spirit to work in you and to live in you? Oh, come and confess every failure of temper, every failure of tongue however small, every failure owing to the absence of the Holy Spirit and the presence of the power of self. Are you consecrated? Are you given up to the Holy Spirit?

If your answer is, "No," then I come with a second question—Are you willing to be consecrated? Are you willing to give up yourself to the power of the Holy Spirit?

You well know that the human side of consecration will not help you. I may consecrate myself a hundred times with all the intensity of my being, and that will not help me. What will help me is this: that God from Heaven accepts and seals the consecration.

And now are you willing to give yourselves up to the Holy Spirit? You can do it now. A great deal may still be dark and dim, and beyond what we understand, and you may feel nothing. But come. God alone can effect the change. God alone, who gave us the Holy Spirit, can restore the Holy Spirit in power into our life. God alone can "strengthen us with might by his Spirit in the inner man." And to every waiting heart that will make the sacrifice and give up everything and give time to cry and pray to God, the answer will come. The blessing is not far off. Our God delights to help us. He will enable us to perfect, not in the flesh, but in the Spirit, what was begun in the Spirit.

Kept by the Power of God

The words from which I speak you will find in 1 Peter 1:5. The third, fourth, and fifth verses are: "Blessed be the God and Father of our Lord Jesus Christ, which . . . has begotten us again unto a lively hope by the resurrection of Jesus Christ from the dead, to an inheritance incorruptible . . . reserved in heaven for you, who are kept by the power of God through faith unto salvation." The words of my text are: "Kept by the power of God through faith."

There we have two wonderful, blessed truths about the keeping by which a believer is kept unto salvation. One truth is, Kept by the power of God. And the other truth is, Kept through faith. We should look at the two sides: at God's side and his almighty power, offered to us to be our Keeper every moment of the day; and at the human side—we having nothing to do but in faith to let God do his keeping work. We are begotten again to an inheritance kept in Heaven for us, and we are kept here on earth by the power of God. We see there is a double keeping—the inheritance kept for me in Heaven, and I on earth kept for the inheritance there.

Now, as to the first part of this keeping, there is no doubt and no question. God keeps the inheritance in Heaven very wonderfully and perfectly, and it is waiting there safely. And the same God keeps me for the inheritance. That is what I want to understand.

You know it is very foolish of a father to take great trouble to have an inheritance for his children and to keep it for them if he does not keep them for it. What would you think of a man spending his whole time and making every sacrifice to amass money, and as he gets his tens of thousands, you ask him why it is that he sacrifices himself so, and his answer is: "I want to leave my children a large inheritance, and I am keeping it for them," if you were then to hear that that man takes no trouble to educate his children, that he allows them to run upon the street wild and to go on in paths of sin and ignorance and folly. What would you think of him? Would not you say: "Poor man! He is keeping an inheritance for his children, but he is not keeping or preparing his children for the inheritance!" And there are so many Christians who think, "My God is keeping the inheritance for me," but they cannot believe, "My God is keeping me for that inheritance." The same power, the same love, the same God doing the double work.

Now, I want to speak about a work God does upon us: keeping us for the inheritance. I have already said that we have two very simple truths: the one the divine side—we are kept by the power of God; the other, the human side—we are kept through faith.

I

Look at the divine side: Christians are kept by the power of God.

Think, first of all, that this keeping is all-inclusive.

What is kept? You are kept. How much of you? The whole being. Does God keep one part of you and not another? No. Some people have an idea that this is a sort of vague, general keeping, and that God will keep them in such a way that when they die they will get to Heaven. But they do not apply that word "kept" to everything in their being and nature. And yet that is what God wants.

Here I have a watch. Suppose that this watch had been borrowed from a friend, and he said to me, "When you go to Europe, I will let you take it with you, but mind you keep it safely and bring it back."

And suppose I damaged the watch, and had the hands broken, and the face defaced, and some of the wheels and springs spoiled, and took it back in that condition, and handed it to my friend. He would say, "Ah, but I gave you that watch on condition that you would keep it."

"Have I not kept it? There is the watch."

"But I did not want you to keep it in that general way, so that you should bring me back only the shell of the watch or the remains. I expected you to keep every part of it."

And so God does not want to keep us in this general way, so that at the last, somehow or other, we shall be saved as by fire, and just get into Heaven. But the keeping power and the love of God applies to every particular of our being.

There are some people who think God will keep them in spiritual things but not in temporal things. This latter, they say, lies outside of his line. Now, God sends you to work in the world, but he did not say: "I must now leave you to go and earn your own money and to get your livelihood for yourself." He knows you are not able to keep yourself. But God says: "My child, there is no work you are to do, and no business in which you are engaged, and not a cent which you are to spend, but I, your Father, will take that up into my keeping." God not only cares for the spiritual but for the temporal, also. The greater part of the life of many people must be spent, sometimes eight or nine or ten hours a day, amid the temptations and distractions of business, but God will care for you there. The keeping of God includes all.

There are other people who think: "Ah, in time of trial God keeps me, but in times of prosperity I do not need his keeping; then I forget him and let him go." Others, again, think the very opposite. They think: "In time of prosperity, when things are smooth and quiet, I am able to cling to God, but when heavy trials come, somehow or other my will rebels, and God does not keep me then."

Now, I bring you the message that in prosperity as in adversity, in the sunshine as in the dark, your God is ready to keep you all the time.

Then again, there are others who think of this keeping thus: "God will keep me from doing very great wickedness, but there are small sins I cannot expect God to keep me from. There is the sin of temper. I cannot expect God to conquer that."

When you hear of some man who has been tempted and gone astray or fallen into drunkenness or murder, you thank God for his keeping power.

"I might have done the same as that man," you say, "if God had not kept me." And you believe he kept you from drunkenness and murder.

And why do you not need believe that God can keep you from out-breaks of temper? You thought that this was of less importance; you did not remember that the great commandment of the New Testament is "Love one another as I have loved you" (John 13:34). And when your temper and hasty judgment and sharp words came out, you sinned against the highest law—the law of God's love. And yet you say, "God will not; God cannot'—no, you will not say, God cannot; but you say, "God does not keep me from that." You perhaps say, "He can, but there is something in me that cannot attain to it and which God does not take away."

I want to ask you, Can believers live a holier life than is generally lived? Can believers experience the keeping power of God all the day to keep them from sin? Can believers be kept in fellowship with God? And I bring you a message from the Word of God, in these words: "Kept by the power of God." There is no qualifying clause to them. The meaning is that if you will entrust yourself entirely and absolutely to the omnipotence of God, he will delight to keep you.

Some people think that they never can get so far as that every word of their mouth should be to the glory of God. But it is what God wants of them; it is what God expects of them. God is willing to set a watch at the door of their mouth, and if God will do that, cannot he keep their tongue and their lips? He can, and that is what God is going to do for them that trust him. God's keeping is all-inclusive, and let everyone who longs to live a holy life think out all their needs and all their weaknesses and all their shortcomings and all their sins, and say deliberately: "Is there any sin that my God cannot keep me from?" And the heart will have to answer: "No; God can keep me from every sin."

Second, if you want to understand this keeping, remember that it is not only an all-inclusive keeping, but it is an almighty keeping.

I want to get that truth burned into my soul; I want to worship God until my whole heart is filled with the thought of his omnipotence. God is almighty, and the Almighty God offers himself to work in my heart, to do the work of keeping me. And I want to get linked with Omnipotence, or rather, linked to the Omnipotent One, to the living God, and to have my place in the hollow of his hand. You read the Psalms, and you think of the wonderful thoughts in many of the expressions that David uses, as, for instance, when he speaks about God being our God, our Fortress, our Refuge, our strong Tower, our Strength and our Salvation. David had very wonderful views of how the everlasting God is himself the hiding place of the believing soul and of how he takes the believer and keeps him in the very hollow of his hand, in the secret of his pavilion, under the shadow of his wings, under his very feathers. And there David lived. And, oh, we who are the children of Pentecost, we who have known Christ and his blood and the Holy Spirit sent down from Heaven—why is it we know so little of what it is to walk tremblingly step by step with the Almighty God as our Keeper?

Have you ever thought that in every action of grace in your heart, you have the whole omnipotence of God engaged to bless you? When I come to a man, and he bestows upon me a gift of money, I get it and go away with it. He has given me something of his; the rest he keeps for himself. But that is not the way with the power of God. God can part with nothing of his own power, and therefore I can experience the power and goodness of God only in so far as I am in contact and fellowship with himself. And when I come into contact and fellowship with himself, I come into contact and fellowship with the whole omnipotence of God, and have the omnipotence of God to help me every day.

A son has, perhaps, a very rich father, and as the former is about to commence business, the father says: "You can have as much money as you want for your undertaking." All the father has is at the disposal of the son. And that is the way with God, your Almighty God. You can hardly take it in; you feel yourself such a little worm. His omnipotence needed to keep a little worm! Yes, his omnipotence is needed to keep every little worm that lives in the dust, and also to keep the universe, and therefore his omnipotence is much more needed in keeping your soul and mine from the power of sin.

Oh, if you want to grow in grace, do learn to begin here. In all your judgings and meditations and thoughts and deeds and questionings and studies and prayers, learn to be kept by your Almighty God. What is Almighty God not going to do for the child that trusts him? The Bible says, "above all that we can ask or think" (Ephesians 3:20). It is Omnipotence you must learn to know and trust, and then you will live as a Christian ought to live. How little we have learned to study God, and to understand that a godly life is a life full of God—a life that loves God and waits on him and trusts him and allows him to bless it! We cannot do the will of God except by the power of God. God gives us the first experience of his power to prepare us to long for more and to come and claim all that he can do. God help us to trust him every day.

Another thought: This keeping is not only all-inclusive and omnipotent, but also continuous and unbroken.

People sometimes say: "For a week or a month God has kept me very wonderfully; I have lived in the light of his countenance, and I cannot say what joy I have not had in fellowship with him. He has blessed me in my work for others. He has given me souls, and at times I felt as if I were carried heavenward on eagle's wings. But it did not continue. It was too good; it could not last." And some say, "It was necessary that I should fall to keep me humble." And others say, "I know it was my own fault; but somehow you cannot always live up in the heights."

Oh, beloved, why is it? Can there be any reason why the keeping of God should not be continuous and unbroken? Just think. All life is in unbroken continuity. If my life were stopped for half an hour, I would be dead, and my life gone. Life is a continuous thing, and the life of God is the life of his Church, and the life of God is his almighty power working in us. And God comes to us as the Almighty One, and without any condition he offers to be my Keeper, and his keeping means that day by day, moment by moment, God is going to keep us.

If I were to ask you the question, "Do you think God is able to keep you one day from actual transgression," you would answer: "I not only know he is able to do it, but I think he has done it. There have been days in which he has kept my heart in his holy presence—when, though I have always had a sinful nature within me, he has kept me from conscious, actual transgression."

Now, if he can do that for an hour or a day, why not for two days? Oh, let us make God's omnipotence as revealed in his Word the measure of our expectations. Has God not said in his Word, "I, the Lord, do keep it, and will water it every moment" (Isaiah 27:3)? What can that mean? Does "every moment" mean every moment? Did God promise of that vineyard of red wine that every moment he would water it so that the heat of the sun and the scorching wind might never dry it up? Yes. In South Africa they sometimes make a graft, and above it they tie a bottle of water so that now and then there shall be a drop to saturate what they have put about it. And so the moisture is kept there unceasingly until the graft has had time to strike and resist the heat of the sun.

Will our God, in his tender-hearted love toward us, not keep us every moment when he has promised to do so? Oh, if we once got hold of the thought, Our whole spiritual life is to be God's doing—"It is God that works in us to will and to do of his good pleasure" (Philippians 2:13). When once we get faith to expect that from God, God will do all for us.

The keeping is to be continuous. Every morning God will meet you as you wake. It is not a question of, If I forgot to wake in the morning with the thought of him, what will come of it? If you trust your waking to God, God will meet you in the morning as you wake with his divine sunshine and love, and he will give you the consciousness, through the day, that you have got God to take charge of you continuously with his almighty power. And God will meet you the next day and every day, and never mind if in the practice of fellowship there comes failure sometimes.

If you maintain your position and say, "Lord, I am going to expect you to do your utmost, and I am going to trust you day by day to keep me absolutely," then your faith will grow stronger and stronger, and you will know the keeping power of God in unbrokenness.

II

And now the other side—believing. "Kept by the power of God through faith." How must we look at this faith?

Let me say, first of all, that this faith means utter impotence and helplessness before God.

At the bottom of all faith there is a feeling of helplessness. If I have a bit of business to transact, perhaps to buy a house, the lawyer must do the work of getting the transfer of the property in my name and making all the arrangements. I cannot do that work, and in trusting that agent I confess I cannot do it. And so faith always means helplessness. In many cases it means that I can do it with a great deal of trouble, but another can do it better. But in most cases it is utter helplessness; another must do it for me. And that is the secret of the spiritual life. A man must learn to say: "I give up everything; I have tried and longed and thought and prayed, but failure has come. God has blessed me and helped me, but still, in the long run, there has been so much of sin and sadness." What a change comes when a man is thus broken down into utter helplessness and self-despair, and says, "I can do nothing!"

Remember Paul. He was living a blessed life, and he had been taken up into the third Heaven, and then the thorn in the flesh came, "a messenger of Satan to buffet me." And what happened? Paul could not understand it, and he prayed the Lord three times to take it away. But the Lord said, in effect, "No; it is possible that you might exalt yourself, and therefore I have sent you this trial to keep you weak and humble."

And Paul then learned a lesson that he never forgot, and that was to rejoice in his infirmities. He said that the weaker he was, the better it was for him, for when he was weak, he was strong in his Lord Christ.

Do you want to enter what people call "the higher life"? Then go a step lower down. I remember Dr. William Boardman telling how once he was invited by a gentleman to go to see a factory where they made fine shot, and I believe the workmen did so by pouring down molten lead from a great height. This gentleman wanted to take Dr. Boardman up to the top of the tower to see how the work was done. The doctor came to the tower, he entered by the door, and began going upstairs. But when he had gone a few steps, the gentleman called out: "That is the wrong way. You must come down this way; that stair is locked up."

The gentleman took him downstairs a good many steps, and there an elevator was ready to take him to the top. And he said: "I have learned a lesson that going down is often the best way to get up."

Ah, yes, God will have to bring us very low down; there will have to come upon us a sense of emptiness and despair and nothingness. It is when we sink down in utter helplessness that the everlasting God will reveal himself in his power, and that our hearts will learn to trust God alone.

What is it that keeps us from trusting him perfectly?

Many a one says: "I believe what you say, but there is one difficulty. If my trust were perfect and always abiding, all would come right, for I know God will honor trust. But how am I to get that trust?"

My answer is: "By the death of self. The great hindrance to trust is self-effort. So long as you have got your own wisdom and thoughts and strength, you cannot fully trust God. But when God breaks you down, when everything begins to grow dim before your eyes and you see that you understand nothing, then God is coming near. And if you will bow down in nothingness and wait upon God, he will become all."

As long as we are something, God cannot be all, and his omnipotence cannot do its full work. That is the beginning of faith—utter despair of self, a ceasing from man and everything on earth, and finding our hope in God alone.

And then, next, we must understand that faith is rest.

In the beginning of the faith-life, faith is struggling. But as long as faith is struggling, faith has not attained its strength. But when faith in its struggling gets to the end of itself and just throws itself upon God and rests on him, then comes joy and victory.

Perhaps I can make it plainer if I tell the story of how the Keswick Convention began. Canon Thomas Harford-Battersby was an evangelical clergyman of the Church of England for more than twenty years, a man of deep and tender godliness, but he had not the consciousness of rest and victory over sin and often was deeply sad at the thought of stumbling and failure and sin. When he heard about the possibility of victory, he felt it was desirable, but it was as if he could not attain it. On one occasion, he heard an address on "Rest and Faith," from the story of the nobleman who came from Capernaum to Cana to ask Christ to heal his child. In the address, it was shown that the nobleman believed that Christ could help him in a general way, but he came to Jesus a good deal by way of an experiment. He hoped Christ would help him, but he had not any assurance of that help. But what happened? When Christ said to him, "Go your way, for your child lives," that man believed the word that Jesus spoke; he rested in that word. He had no proof that his child was well again, and he had to walk back seven hours' journey to Capernaum. He walked back, and on the way met his servant and got the first news that the child was well—that at one o'clock on the afternoon of the previous day, at the very time that Jesus spoke to him, the fever left the child. That father rested upon the word of Jesus and his work, and he went down to Capernaum and found his child well. And he praised God and became, with his whole house, a believer and disciple of Jesus.

Oh, friends, that is faith! When God comes to me with the promise of his keeping, and I have nothing on earth to trust in, I say to God: "Your word is enough; kept by the power of God." That is faith; that is rest.

When Canon Battersby heard that address, he went home that night and in the darkness of the night found rest. He rested on the word of Jesus. And the next morning, in the streets of Oxford, he said to a friend: "I have found it!" Then he went and told others and asked that the Keswick Convention might be begun, and that those at the convention with himself should testify simply what God had done.

It is a great thing when a man comes to rest on God's almighty power for every moment of his life, in prospect of temptations to temper and haste and anger and unlovingness and pride and sin. It is a great thing in prospect of these to enter into a covenant with the omnipotent Jehovah, not on account of anything that any man says, or of anything that my heart feels, but on the strength of the Word of God: "Kept by the power of God through faith."

Oh, let us say to God that we are going to test him to the very uttermost. Let us say: "We ask you for nothing more than you can give, but we want nothing less." Let us say: "My God, let my life be a proof of what the omnipotent God can do. Let these be the two dispositions of our souls every day: deep helplessness, and simple, childlike rest.

That brings me to just one more thought in regard to faith: Faith implies fellowship with God.

Many people want to take the Word and believe that, and they find they cannot believe it. Ah, no, you cannot separate God from his Word. No goodness or power can be received separate from God, and if you want to get into this life of godliness, you must take time for fellowship with God.

People sometimes tell me, "My life is one of such scurry and bustle that I have no time for fellowship with God." A dear missionary said to me: "People do not know how we missionaries are tempted. I get up at five o'clock in the morning, and there are the natives waiting for their orders for work. Then I have to go to the school and spend hours there. And then there is other work, and sixteen hours rush along, and I hardly get time to be alone with God."

Ah, there is the lack. I pray you, remember two things. I have not told you to trust the omnipotence of God as a thing, and I have not told you to trust the Word of God as a written book, but I have told you to go to the God of omnipotence and the God of the Word. Deal with God as that nobleman dealt with the living Christ. Why was he able to believe the word that Christ spoke to him? Because in the very eyes and tones and voice of Jesus, the Son of God, he saw and heard something which made him feel that he could trust him. And that is what Christ can do for you and me. Do not try to stir and arouse faith from within. How often I have tried to do that, and made a fool of myself! You cannot stir up faith from the depths of your heart. Leave your heart, and look into the face of Christ, and listen to what he tells you about how he will keep you. Look up into the face of your loving Father, and take time every day with him, and begin a new life with the deep emptiness and poverty of a man who has got nothing and who wants to get everything from him—with the deep restfulness of a man who rests on the living God, the omnipotent Jehovah—and try God, and prove him if he will not open the windows of Heaven and pour out a blessing that there shall not be room to receive it.

I close by asking if you are willing to experience to the very full the heavenly keeping for the heavenly inheritance? Robert Murray M'Cheyne says somewhere, "O God, make me as holy as a pardoned sinner can be made." And if that prayer is in your heart, come now, and let us enter into a covenant with the everlasting and omnipotent Jehovah afresh, and in great helplessness, but in great restfulness, place ourselves in his hands. And then as we enter into our covenant, let us have the one prayer—that we may believe fully that the everlasting God is going to be our Companion, holding our hand every moment of the day; our Keeper, watching over us without a moment's interval; our Father, delighting to reveal himself in our souls always. He has the power to let the sunshine of his love be with us all the day. Do not be afraid because you have got your business that you cannot have God with you always. Learn the lesson that the natural sun shines upon you all the day, and you enjoy its light, and wherever you are, you have got the sun; God takes care that it shines upon you. And God will take care that his own divine light shines upon you, and that you shall abide in that light, if you will only trust him for it. Let us trust God to do that with a great and entire trust.

Here is the omnipotence of God, and here is faith reaching out to the measure of that omnipotence. Shall we not say: "All that that omnipotence can do, I am going to trust my God for"? Are not the two sides of this heavenly life wonderful? God's omnipotence covers me, and my will in its littleness rests in that omnipotence, and rejoices in it!

> *Moment by moment, I'm kept in his love;*
> *Moment by moment, I've life from above;*
> *Looking to Jesus, the glory does shine;*
> *Moment by moment, Oh, Lord, I am thine!*

You Are the Branches

Everything depends on our being right ourselves in Christ. If I want good apples, I must have a good apple tree, and if I care for the health of the apple tree, the apple tree will give me good apples. And it is just so with our Christian life and work. If our life with Christ be right, all will come right. There may be the need of instruction and suggestion and help and training in the different departments of the work; all that has value. But in the long run, the greatest essential is to have the full life in Christ—in other words, to have Christ in us, working through us. I know how much there often is to disturb us or to cause anxious questionings But the Master has such a blessing for every one of us, and such perfect peace and rest, and such joy and strength, if we can only come into, and be kept in, the right attitude toward him.

I will take my text from the parable of the vine and the branches in John 15:5: "I am the vine, you are the branches." Especially these words: "You are the branches."

What a simple thing it is to be a branch, the branch of a tree or the branch of a vine! The branch grows out of the vine or out of the tree, and there it lives and grows and, in due time, bears fruit. It has no responsibility except just to receive from the root and stem sap and nourishment. And if we only by the Holy Spirit knew our relationship to Jesus Christ, our work would be changed into the brightest and most heavenly thing upon earth. Instead of there ever being soul-weariness or exhaustion, our work would be like a new experience, linking us to Jesus as nothing else can. For, alas, is it not often true that our work comes between us and Jesus? What folly! The very work that he has to do in me, and I for him, I take up in such a way that it separates me from Christ. Many a laborer in the vineyard has complained that he has too much work and no time for close communion with Jesus, and that his usual work weakens his inclination for prayer, and that his too much intercourse with men darkens the spiritual life. Sad thought, that the bearing of fruit should separate the branch from the vine! That must be because we have looked upon our work as something other than the branch bearing fruit. May God deliver us from every false thought about the Christian life.

Now, just a few thoughts about this blessed branch-life.

In the first place, it is a life of absolute dependence. The branch has nothing; it just depends upon the vine for everything. Absolute dependence is one of the most solemn and precious of thoughts. A great German theologian wrote two large volumes some years ago to show that the whole of Calvin's theology is summed up in that one principle of absolute dependence upon God—and he was right. Another great writer has said that absolute, unalterable dependence upon God alone is the essence of the religion of angels and should be that of men, also. God is everything to the angels, and he is willing to be everything to the Christian. If I can learn every moment of the day to depend upon God, everything will come right. You will get the higher life if you depend absolutely upon God.

Now, here we find it with the vine and the branches. Every vine you ever see, or every bunch of grapes that comes upon your table, let it remind you that the branch is absolutely dependent on the vine. The vine has to do the work, and the branch enjoys the fruit of it.

What has the vine to do? It has to do a great work. It has to send its roots out into the soil and hunt under the ground—the roots often extend a long way out—for nourishment, and to drink in the moisture. Put certain elements of manure in certain directions, and the vine sends its roots there, and then in its roots or stems it turns the moisture and manure into that special sap which is to make the fruit that is borne. The vine does the work, and the branch has just to receive from the vine the sap, which is changed into grapes. I have been told that at Hampton Court, London, there is a vine that sometimes bore a couple of thousand bunches of grapes, and people were astonished at its large growth and rich fruitage. Afterward it was discovered what was the cause of it. Not so very far away runs the River Thames, and the vine had stretched its roots away hundreds of yards under the ground until it had come to the riverside, and there in all the rich slime of the riverbed it had found rich nourishment and obtained moisture, and the roots had drawn the sap all that distance up and up into the vine, and as a result there was the abundant, rich harvest. The vine had the work to do, and the branches had just to depend upon the vine and receive what it gave.

Is that literally true of my Lord Jesus? Must I understand that when I have to work, when I have to preach a sermon or address a Bible class or to go out and visit the poor, neglected ones, that all the responsibility of the work is on Christ?

That is exactly what Christ wants you to understand. Christ wants that in all your work, the very foundation should be the simple, blessed consciousness: Christ must care for all.

And how does he fulfill the trust of that dependence? He does it by sending down the Holy Spirit—not now and then only as a special gift, for remember the relationship between the vine and the branches is such that hourly, daily, unceasingly there is the living connection maintained. The sap does not flow for a time and then stop and then flow again, but from moment to moment the sap flows from the vine to the branches. And just so, my Lord Jesus wants me to take that blessed position as a worker, and morning by morning and day by day and hour by hour and step by step, in every work I have to go out to just to abide before him in the simple, utter helplessness of one who knows nothing and is nothing and can do nothing. Oh, beloved workers, study that word "nothing." You sometimes sing, "Oh, to be nothing, nothing." But have you really studied that word and prayed every day and worshipped God in the light of it? Do you know the blessedness of that word "nothing"?

If I am something, then God is not everything. But when I become nothing, God can become all, and the everlasting God in Christ can reveal himself fully. That is the higher life. We need to become nothing. Someone has well said that the seraphim and cherubim are flames of fire because they know they are nothing, and they allow God to put his fullness and his glory and brightness into them. Oh, become nothing in deep reality, and, as a worker, study only one thing: to become poorer and lower and more helpless, that Christ may work all in you.

Workers, here is your first lesson: learn to be nothing; learn to be helpless. The man who has got something is not absolutely dependent, but the man who has got nothing is absolutely dependent. Absolute dependence upon God is the secret of all power in work. The branch has nothing but what it gets from the vine, and you and I can have nothing but what we get from Jesus.

But second, the life of the branch is not only a life of entire dependence, but of deep restfulness.

That little branch, if it could think, and if it could feel, and if it could speak—that branch away in Hampton Court vine, or on some of the million vines that we have in South Africa, in our sunny land—if we could have a little branch here today to talk to us, and if we could say, "Come, branch of the vine, I want to learn from you how I can be a true branch of the living Vine," what would it answer? The little branch would whisper: "Man, I hear that you are wise, and I know that you can do a great many wonderful things. I know you have much strength and wisdom given to you, but I have one lesson for you. With all your hurry and effort in Christ's work, you never prosper. The first thing you need is to come and rest in your Lord Jesus. That is what I do. Since I grew out of that vine, I have spent years and years, and all I have done is just to rest in the vine. When the time of spring came, I had no anxious thought or care. The vine began to pour its sap into me and to give the bud and leaf. And when the time of summer came, I had no care, and in the great heat I trusted the vine to bring moisture to keep me fresh. And in the time of harvest, when the owner came to pluck the grapes, I had no care. If there was anything in the grapes not good, the owner never blamed the branch; the blame was always on the vine. And if you would be a true branch of Christ, the living Vine, just rest on him. Let Christ bear the responsibility."

You say, "Won't that make me slothful?"

I tell you it will not. No one who learns to rest upon the living Christ can become slothful, for the closer your contact with Christ, the more of the Spirit of his zeal and love will be borne in upon you. But, oh, begin to work in the midst of your entire dependence by adding to that deep restfulness. A man sometimes tries and tries to be dependent upon Christ, but he worries himself about this absolute dependence; he tries and he cannot get it. But let him sink down into entire restfulness every day.

> In your strong hand I lay me down.
> So shall the work be done;
> For who can work so wondrously
> As the Almighty One?

Worker, take your place every day at the feet of Jesus in the blessed peace and rest that come from the knowledge:

I have no care, my cares are his!
I have no fear, he cares for all my fears.

Come, children of God, and understand that it is the Lord Jesus who wants to work through you. You complain of the lack of fervent love. It will come from Jesus. He will give the divine love in your heart with which you can love people. That is the meaning of the assurance, "The love of God is shed abroad in our hearts by the Holy Spirit" (Romans 5:5), and of that other word, "The love of Christ constrains us" (2 Corinthians 5:14). Christ can give you a fountain of love so that you cannot help loving the most wretched and the most ungrateful, or those who have wearied you hitherto. Rest in Christ, who can give wisdom and strength, and you do not know how that restfulness will often prove to be the very best part of your message. You plead with people and you argue, and they get the idea: "There is a man arguing and striving with me." They only feel, "Here are two men dealing with each other." But if you will let the deep rest of God come over you, the rest in Christ Jesus, the peace and rest and holiness of Heaven, that restfulness will bring a blessing to the heart, even more than the words you speak.

But third, the branch teaches a lesson of much fruitfulness.

The Lord Jesus Christ repeated that word "fruit" often in that parable. He spoke, first, of fruit, and then of more fruit, and then of much fruit. Yes, you are ordained not only to bear fruit, but to bear much fruit. "Herein is my Father glorified, that you bear much fruit" (John 15:8). In the first place, Christ said: "I am the Vine, and my Father is the Husbandman. My Father is the Husbandman who has charge of me and you." He who will watch over the connection between Christ and the branches is God, and it is in the power of God through Christ we are to bear fruit.

Oh, Christians, you know this world is perishing for the want of workers. And it lacks not only more workers—the workers are saying, some more earnestly than others: "We need not only more workers, but we need our workers to have a new power, a different life—that we workers should be able to bring more blessing." Children of God, I appeal to you. You know what trouble you take, say, in a case of sickness. You have a beloved friend apparently in danger of death, and nothing can refresh that friend so much as a few grapes, and they are out of season. But what trouble you will take to get the grapes that are to be the nourishment of this dying friend! And, oh, there are around you people who never go to church, and so many who go to church but do not know Christ. And yet the heavenly grapes, the grapes of the heavenly Vine, are not to be had at any price, except as the child of God bears them out of his inner life in fellowship with Christ. Except the children of God are filled with the sap of the heavenly Vine, except they are filled with the Holy Spirit and the love of Jesus, they cannot bear much of the real heavenly grape. We all confess there is a great deal of work, a great deal of preaching and teaching and visiting, a great deal of machinery, a great deal of earnest effort of every kind—but there is not much manifestation of the power of God in it.

What is lacking? There is lacking the close connection between the worker and the heavenly Vine. Christ, the heavenly Vine, has blessings that he could pour on tens of thousands who are perishing. Christ, the heavenly Vine, has power to provide the heavenly grapes. But "you are the branches," and you cannot bear heavenly fruit unless you are in close connection with Jesus Christ.

Do not confound work and fruit. There may be a good deal of work for Christ that is not the fruit of the heavenly Vine. Do not seek for work only. Oh, study this question of fruit-bearing. It means the very life and the very power and the very spirit and the very love within the heart of the Son of God; it means the heavenly Vine himself coming into your heart and mine.

You know there are different sorts of grapes, each with a different name, and every vine provides exactly that peculiar aroma and juice which gives the grape its particular flavor and taste. Just so, there is in the heart of Christ Jesus a life and a love and a Spirit and a blessing and a power for men that are entirely heavenly and divine, and that will come down into our hearts. Stand in close connection with the heavenly Vine and say: "Lord Jesus, nothing less than the sap that flows through yourself, nothing less than the Spirit of your divine life, is what we ask. Lord Jesus, I pray you, let your Spirit flow through me in all my work for you."

I tell you again that the sap of the heavenly Vine is nothing but the Holy Spirit. The Holy Spirit is the life of the heavenly Vine, and what you must get from Christ is nothing less than a strong inflow of the Holy Spirit. You need it exceedingly, and you want nothing more than that. Remember that. Do not expect Christ to give a bit of strength here, and a bit of blessing yonder, and a bit of help over there. As the vine does its work in giving its own peculiar sap to the branch, so expect Christ to give his own Holy Spirit into your heart, and then you will bear much fruit. And if you have only begun to bear fruit, and are listening to the word of Christ in the parable, "more fruit," "much fruit," remember that in order that you should bear more fruit you just require more of Jesus in your life and heart.

We ministers of the Gospel, how we are in danger of getting into a condition of "work, work, work"! And we pray over it, but the freshness and buoyancy and joy of the heavenly life are not always present. Let us seek to understand that the life of the branch is a life of much fruit, because it is a life rooted in Christ, the living, heavenly Vine.

And fourth, the life of the branch is a life of close communion. Let us again ask: What has the branch to do? You know that precious, inexhaustible word that Christ used: "Abide." Your life is to be an abiding life. And how is the abiding to be? It is to be just like the branch in the vine, abiding every minute of the day. There are the branches in close communion, in unbroken communion, with the vine from January to December. And cannot I live every day—it is to me an almost terrible thing that we should ask the question—cannot I live in abiding communion with the heavenly Vine?

You say: "But I am so much occupied with other things."

You may have ten hours' hard work daily, during which your brain has to be occupied with temporal things; God orders it so. But the abiding work is the work of the heart, not of the brain, the work of the heart clinging to and resting in Jesus, a work in which the Holy Spirit links us to Christ Jesus. Oh, do believe that deeper down than the brain, deep down in the inner life, you can abide in Christ, so that every moment you are free the consciousness will come, "Blessed Jesus, I am still in you."

If you will learn for a time to put aside other work and to get into this abiding contact with the heavenly Vine, you will find that fruit will come.

What is the application to our life of this abiding communion? What does it mean?

It means close fellowship with Christ in secret prayer. I am sure there are Christians who do long for the higher life, and who sometimes have got a great blessing and have at times found a great inflow of heavenly joy and a great outflow of heavenly gladness, and yet after a time it has passed away. They have not understood that close personal actual communion with Christ is an absolute necessity for daily life. Take time to be alone with Christ. Nothing in Heaven or earth can free you from the necessity for that if you are to be happy and holy Christians.

Oh, how many Christians look upon it as a burden and a tax and a duty and a difficulty to be often alone with God! That is the great hindrance to our Christian life everywhere. We need more quiet fellowship with God, and I tell you in the name of the heavenly Vine that you cannot be healthy branches, branches into which the heavenly sap can flow, unless you take plenty of time for communion with God. If you are not willing to sacrifice time to get alone with him, and to give him time every day to work in you and to keep up the link of connection between you and himself, he cannot give you that blessing of his unbroken fellowship. Jesus Christ asks you to live in close communion with him. Let every heart say: "O Christ, it is this I long for; it is this I choose." And he will gladly give it to you.

And then finally, the life of the branch is a life of absolute surrender.

These words, "absolute surrender," are great and solemn words, and I believe we do not understand their meaning. But yet the little branch preaches it.

"Have you anything to do, little branch, besides bearing grapes?"

"No, nothing."

"Are you fit for nothing?"

Fit for nothing! The Bible says that a bit of vine cannot even be used as a pen; it is fit for nothing but to be burned.

"And now, what do you understand, little branch, about your relationship to the vine?"

"My relationship is just this: I am utterly given up to the vine, and the vine can give me as much or as little sap as it chooses. Here I am at its disposal and the vine can do with me what it likes."

Oh, friends, we need this absolute surrender to the Lord Jesus Christ. The more I speak, the more I feel that this is one of the most difficult points to make clear and one of the most important and needful points to explain—what this absolute surrender is.

It is often an easy thing for a man or woman to come out and offer themselves up to God for entire consecration, and to say: "Lord, it is my desire to give up myself entirely to you." That is of great value, and often brings very rich blessing. But the one question I ought to study quietly is, What is meant by absolute surrender?

It means that, as literally as Christ was given up entirely to God, I am given up entirely to Christ. Is that too strong? Some think so. Some think that never can be—that just as entirely and absolutely as Christ gave up his life to do nothing but seek the Father's pleasure, and to depend on the Father absolutely and entirely, I am to do nothing but to seek the pleasure of Christ. But that is actually true. Christ Jesus came to breathe his own Spirit into us, to make us find our very highest happiness in living entirely for God, just as he did. Oh, beloved brethren, if that is the case, then I ought to say: "Yes, as true as it is of that little branch of the vine, so true, by God's grace, I would have it to be of me. I would live day by day that Christ may be able to do with me what he will."

Ah, here comes the terrible mistake that lies at the bottom of so much of our own religion. A man thinks: "I have my business and family duties and my relationships as a citizen, and all this I cannot change. And now alongside all this I am to take in religion and the service of God as something that will keep me from sin. God help me to perform my duties properly!"

This is not right. When Christ came, he came and bought the sinner with his blood. If there were a slave market here, and I were to buy a slave, I should take that slave away to my own house from his old surroundings, and he would live at my house as my personal property, and I could order him about all the day. And if he were a faithful slave, he would live as having no will and no interests of his own, his one care being to promote the well-being and honor of his master. And in like manner I, who have been bought with the blood of Christ, have been bought to live every day with the one thought, How can I please my Master?

Oh, we find the Christian life so difficult because we seek for God's blessing while we live in our own will. We should be glad to live the Christian life according to our own liking. We make our own plans and choose our own work, and then we ask the Lord Jesus to come in and take care that sin shall not conquer us too much, and that we shall not go too far wrong; we ask him to come in and give us so much of his blessing. But our relationship to Jesus ought to be such that we are entirely at his disposal and every day come to him humbly and straightforwardly and say: "Lord, is there anything in me that is not according to your will, that has not been ordered by you, or that is not entirely given up to you?"

Oh, if we would wait and wait patiently, I tell you what the result would be. There would spring up a relationship between us and Christ so close and so tender that we should afterward be amazed at how we formerly could have lived with the idea, "I am surrendered to Christ." We should feel how far distant our intercourse with him had previously

been, and that he can, and does indeed, come and take actual possession of us and gives unbroken fellowship all the day. The branch calls
us to absolute surrender.

I do not speak now so much about the giving up of sins. There are
people who need that, people who have got violent tempers, bad habits,
and actual sins which they from time to time commit, and which they
have never given up into the very bosom of the Lamb of God. I pray
you, if you are branches of the living Vine, do not keep one sin back. I
know there are a great many difficulties about this question of holiness.
I know that all do not think exactly the same with regard to it. That
would be to me a matter of comparative indifference if I could see that
all are honestly longing to be free from every sin. But I am afraid that
unconsciously there are in hearts often compromises with the idea that
we cannot be without sin, we must sin a little every day; we cannot help
it. Oh, that people would actually cry to God: "Lord, keep me from sin!"
Give yourself utterly to Jesus, and ask him to do his very utmost for you
in keeping you from sin.

There is a great deal in our work, in our church, and in our surroundings that we found in the world when we were born into it, and it has
grown all around us, and we think that it is all right; it cannot be changed.
We do not come to the Lord Jesus and ask him about it. Oh, I advise you,
Christians, bring everything into relationship with Jesus and say, "Lord,
everything in my life has to be in most complete harmony with my position as a branch of you, the blessed Vine."

Let your surrender to Christ be absolute. I do not understand that word
"surrender" fully; it gets new meanings every now and then; it enlarges
immensely from time to time. But I advise you to speak it out: "Absolute
surrender to you, O Christ, is what I have chosen." And Christ will show
you what is not according to his mind and lead you on to deeper and
higher blessedness.

In conclusion, let me gather up all in one sentence. Christ Jesus said:
"I am the Vine, you are the branches." In other words: "I, the living One
who have so completely given myself to you, am the Vine. You cannot
trust me too much. I am the Almighty Worker, full of a divine life and
power." You are the branches of the Lord Jesus Christ. If there is in your
heart the consciousness that you are not a strong, healthy, fruit-bearing
branch, not closely linked with Jesus, not living in him as you should be,
then listen to him say: "I am the Vine; I will receive you; I will draw you to

myself; I will bless you; I will strengthen you; I will fill you with my Spirit. I, the Vine, have taken you to be my branches; I have given myself utterly to you; children, give yourselves utterly to me. I have surrendered myself as God absolutely to you; I became man and died for you that I might be entirely yours. Come and surrender yourselves entirely to be mine."

What shall our answer be? Oh, let it be a prayer from the depths of our heart that the living Christ may take each one of us and link us close to himself. Let our prayer be that he, the living Vine, shall so link each of us to himself that we shall go away with our hearts singing: "He is my Vine, and I am his branches; I want nothing more; now I have the everlasting Vine." Then when you get alone with him, worship and adore him, praise and trust him, love him and wait for his love. "You are my Vine, and I am your branch. It is enough; my soul is satisfied."

Glory to his blessed name!

CPSIA information can be obtained at www.ICGtesting.com
Printed in the USA
LVOW06s1031060214

372610LV00003B/116/P